P9-DWX-636

Needleweaving

. . . EASY AS EMBROIDERY

by Esther Warner Dendel

Distributed to the trade by
Doubleday & Company, Inc.
Garden City, New York

COUNTRYSIDE PRESS
a division of Farm Journal, Inc.
Philadelphia

Book design: Ann Churchman, Al J. Reagan
Black/white photos: Lee Payne and Jo Dendel—except
    3, 25, 29, 77 Al Reagan; 93 I. Serisawa;
    96, 157 Joan Coverdale;
    104, 114 Jean Stange; 115, 167, 168 Ed Walter
Color photos: Jo Dendel—except 9, 15 Al Reagan;
    10 Ed Walter; 13 I. Serisawa
Drawings: Jean Stange, Associate Professor of Decorative Arts,
    Arizona State University
Library of Congress Catalog Card Number: 77-187033

Copyright © 1971, 1972 by Esther Warner Dendel
Published by Countryside Press
  a division of Farm Journal, Inc.
Distributed to the trade by
  Doubleday & Company, Inc.
  Garden City, New York
All rights reserved
Printed in the United States of America

Needleweaving

...EASY AS EMBROIDERY

by Esther Warner Dendel

Distributed to the trade by
Doubleday & Company, Inc.
Garden City, New York

COUNTRYSIDE PRESS
a division of Farm Journal, Inc.
Philadelphia

Book design: Ann Churchman, Al J. Reagan
Black/white photos: Lee Payne and Jo Dendel—except
     3, 25, 29, 77 Al Reagan; 93 I. Serisawa;
     96, 157 Joan Coverdale;
     104, 114 Jean Stange; 115, 167, 168 Ed Walter
Color photos: Jo Dendel—except 9, 15 Al Reagan;
     10 Ed Walter; 13 I. Serisawa
Drawings: Jean Stange, Associate Professor of Decorative Arts,
     Arizona State University
Library of Congress Catalog Card Number: 77-187033

Copyright © 1971, 1972 by Esther Warner Dendel
Published by Countryside Press
  a division of Farm Journal, Inc.
Distributed to the trade by
  Doubleday & Company, Inc.
  Garden City, New York
All rights reserved
Printed in the United States of America

Contents

A new way to weave

Perhaps we should say that this book tells you how to weave with a new kind of *loom*, because a piece of cardboard actually becomes your "loom". With a curved needle and almost any kind of yarn—plus Nature's offerings such as twigs, feathers, even seaweed—you can start this new craft.

Needleweaving is one of the most flexible and inexpensive of creative crafts. You can do the simplest weaving, or you can develop your artistic abilities as far as they will take you. You might even call this a free-wheeling art form because it is so versatile and personal. It is an adaptation of the ancient craft of weaving that is fast becoming a popular medium of self-expression and pleasure.

Needleweaving is satisfying because you can share your creations in many forms. You can weave decorative accessories for your home, for your wardrobe, make gifts for friends, toys for children, Christmas tree ornaments . . . you can even weave greeting cards for very special people.

In this book you will find so much more than the techniques, although they are all here, step by step. (The artist-craftsman-author, Esther Dendel, is a teacher as well; she and her husband Jo, who shares her enthusiasms, instruct students of all ages in needleweaving and other craft media.) Because of the kind of persons they are, you will find their philosophy of earth's "friendship offerings" woven throughout the book. Mrs. Dendel says: "The home of a craft lies deep in the soul. . . ."

Even if you never put a strand of weft through warp, this book is bound to make you more aware of "art in everyday experience". In fact, Mrs. Dendel authored a book by that title.

Her own awareness had its beginnings on an Iowa farm. Later she was influenced by West Virginia mountain folk and African tribal craftsmen. She lived and worked with both of these peoples who had weaving as one of their basic crafts.

We believe this a unique book that can enrich your life and bring you a new adventure.

RACHEL MARTENS
Crafts/Home Furnishings Editor
Farm Journal

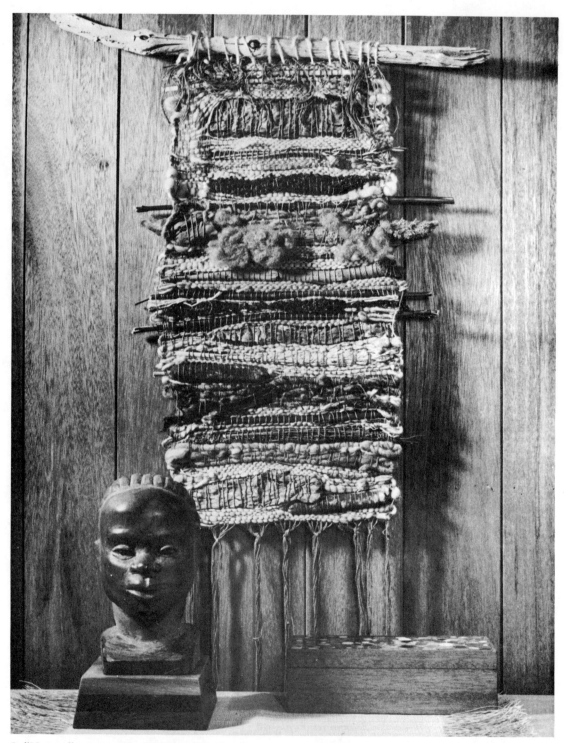

1. "Nature" tapestry by Virginia Weeks shows an appreciation
for things of the earth—cattails, seeds, lichen, tree bark, twigs,
driftwood and palm spathes are all woven into this wall hanging.

1
Why Weave?

Weavers will tell you that it is fun to weave. It is. But the delight of needleweaving goes deeper. Perhaps pleasure more nearly describes the feeling that goes with the work because pleasure and creativity are closely related. "With pleasure, life is a creative adventure; without pleasure it is a struggle for survival," Dr. Alexander Lowen observes in his book on *Pleasure.*

A large part of the pleasure of weaving comes from the fact that a weaver can make up his own rules as he goes along. The weaving thread follows the whim of the weaver as it meanders freely over the surface. You are not really creating if the rules have already been made by another. This is why stamped patterns (like games already made up) are less exciting.

Another great thing about needleweaving is that you can turn dreary time into play time—those hours spent under the hair dryer, waiting in a doctor's office or sitting outside the music room while your youngster has a piano lesson.

You probably glance at the clock and tap a nervous, impatient toe as your mind ticks off all those things still to be accomplished before the day is done. Waiting time is dreary and seems a waste. But not if you have some fulfilling handwork beside you. And there is a great difference here between fulfilling and time-filling.

Needleweaving can be carried about, transported to camp, beach, beauty shop or committee meeting. Chances are you won't notice how dull a meeting is when you're busy with your needle, and everyone around you will wish she were weaving, too! I once carried my needleweaving into a hotel lobby to wait for a friend and in five minutes I was teaching an impromptu class of people lured by the bright yarns.

A few years ago, I slipped on seaweed while photographing tide pools on the Big Sur coast of northern California. The nicest thing my husband brought me in the hospital was a cardboard loom and some yarn. When I remember

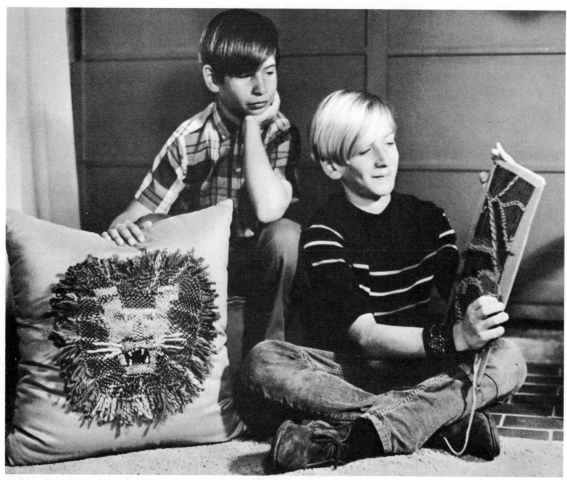

2. *Needleweaving is a hobby for all ages. Mike Hudson, age 12, designer and weaver of the lion pillow, shows his brother David, age 10, the wall hanging he is weaving on a cardboard loom.*

the year I was confined to a wheelchair following that accident, I recall my pleasure in all the needleweaving I did, not the misfortune of a broken leg. A year that might have seemed lost was in fact a year of personal growth and rewarding accomplishments with needle and yarn. I could not, of course, have used a conventional loom. The cardboard was light and fitted across the arms of my wheelchair and I worked in comfort.

There is a rhythm to the over and under, the in and out of needleweaving. When a weaver finds his natural speed, the rhythm that is right for his own body, muscular tensions relax. Breathing, heartbeat, finger motion, a general physical feeling of well-being, all produce pleasure. Some would call this "therapy" (and it is) but I think "pleasure" is the nicer word.

Other people tell me needleweaving helps keep arthritic fingers nimble and in working condition. The yarns are soft and pliable and weaving is indeed a gentle art. It is satisfying for people in rest homes and convalescent homes; patients are sometimes able to sell their work. One woman who does not have any real need for money told me she had sold a needleweaving. Someone was willing to pay money for something she had made and she felt that she was not useless. How happy that made her feel!

To choose and use color is an outgoing action which confirms your self as a unique individual. You will, as you select the colors for your needleweaving, react to each color separately as you hold it in your hand; and to the group of colors acting upon each other when they are assembled. By letting your emotional response have full play, you will have provided an opportunity for personal growth.

Needleweaving is also a way to personalize and individualize your home in these days of look-alike houses on tracts. You may say, "*I* made that" or "I *made* that." Whichever your emphasis, you are making a statement about pleasure you have experienced in the doing—and will continue to have in the looking.

A needlewoven hanging is less likely to appear machine-made than a weaving done on a conventional loom. The cardboard or hardboard (untempered masonite) loom gives great flexibility to the woven product. So it is easier to do something spontaneous and imaginative in needleweaving than in regular weaving.

Another advantage of needleweaving over the conventional loom is the ease of storage. There is no room in the average home for a large loom.

And, finally, everyone can afford this type of "loom" for needleweaving—cardboard costs little or nothing and the hardboard for a 3x4′ loom with leftover scraps for smaller looms costs a mere $1.25.

3. "Leather and Feathers" by Annabelle Bergstrom is a decorative neckpiece done in pheasant colors. It uses the plain weave only, but has 12 different weights, textures and tones of yarns—plus the bits of leather thongs and pheasant feathers.

4. "Sculpture in the Round" by Phil Freeman uses two wooden hoops at an angle to each other. He attached warp top and bottom to yarn wrapped around the hoops; drilled holes for warp on inside curve.

Encourage the men in your family to try needleweaving if they seem intrigued; it is a creative adventure for the whole family together (Plate 2). Fortunately, men are feeling more secure about trying some of the home arts. A former football player of national fame shows off his needlepoint (a close relative of needleweaving) on TV talk shows, and it seems unlikely that anyone is going to call him a sissy. In many cultures men do all the weaving and there is no reason why men in our culture should forego this pleasure.

Young people who want to express individuality in their personal appearance can—with a needle, a bit of cardboard, some jute, fishing line or leather thong, a few feathers, driftwood or sea shells—improvise body coverings and collars that are minor works of art. Annabelle Bergstrom's "Leather and Feathers" (Plate 3) and Virginia Weeks' "Nature" wall hanging (Plate 1) are examples.

Like most of the weavers whose work appears in this book, Annabelle and Virginia are members of our Craft Fellowship. At informal meetings all year, we work toward our annual Craftsmen's Fair which now attracts customers by the thousands. We exhibit our own works, and also invite other craftsmen in the area to participate.

Happily for craftsmen, an increasing number of art associations throughout the country hold Crafts Fairs. Little Galleries are springing up like mushrooms and are looking for the unique crafts products.

There are other encouraging signs. Architects and interior designers visit our fair to choose one-of-a-kind hangings for their clients. Doctors and dentists come looking for something distinctive for their offices. Women who have not yet tried needleweaving themselves, buy hangings to decorate their homes. As each customer admires and touches a needlewoven wall-hanging, we can sense his pleasure in the luminous colors of yarn, the exciting textures of knots and loops, his satisfaction in bringing a well-done craft into his life and into his home.

Some of our weavings are choice, jewel-like little panels no larger than twelve inches. Others are twelve feet long—truly important decorations for lobbies and two-story halls. Many weavers of today are moving their work out from the walls, creating forms which can be viewed from both sides and in the round (Plate 4). Regardless of the size or purpose of the weavings, I feel that their greatest value lies in what the weaving has done for the weaver. This is the real answer to the question, "Why weave?"

5. *Stuffed pillow dolls in all sizes and colors hang as mobiles— woven by Beverly Nemetz.*

2
What to Weave

A belt, a collar, a necklace, a yoke,
A purse, a pillow, a carrying poke;

A greeting for someone special you like,
A blanket in squares for a little tyke;

A mobile to turn in the fitful breeze,
Unusual ornaments for Christmas trees;

A patch, a pocket, a band for a hat,
A room divider, a tie or a mat;

A circle to mark the sliding glass door,
And squares sewed into a rug for the floor;

Something unusual to hang on the wall . . .
You never reach the end or the all.

I often find myself humming as I weave. The rhythm and repetition of "under and over and on to the end" is a healing and pleasureful activity. As you see, it even prompts jingle-making.

And when your project is finished, you can proudly say, "I wove that." *What* one weaves is not as important as that one *does* weave, but this knowledge becomes a certainty only after you have mastered the technique of weaving.

Some people deny themselves the pleasure because they fear they do not have the patience to weave. Instead of soothing their shattered nerves, they are afraid weaving would fray them further.

Fortunately, there are big yarns and coarse fibers that work up quickly and with good effect. They are perfect for people who want things to move fast, or for children whose little

6. *A belt in purples and pinks by Judy Whelan.*

7. *A collar in oranges and browns with copper beads by Judy Whelan.*

14

hands are not yet educated for fine work. Large yarns are no less beautiful for being rough and sturdy, and they certainly help the beginning weaver through the "getting involved" stage. Pleasure in your first small success in weaving deepens as you find you've actually "grown a little patience" too.

I do not believe that anyone is born with patience. I think patience is something each of us has to teach himself. We do well to compel ourselves, if need be, to do certain things which in the beginning, before we have mastered them, require a measure of patience. This pays great dividends as you grow older and find your physical energy in somewhat shorter supply. When life presents problems, the fortunate person is he who "can weave trouble away."

Once you have mastered a craft, you wonder why you thought in the beginning that it required patience. As soon as you find the rhythm of work and adjust it to your own body rhythms of heartbeat and breath, time flies. What seems like half an hour, providing you are conscious at all of time passing, will turn out to be three hours at least. Hunger and fatigue do not intrude. There is only the joy of the work. That is what is meant by being involved. The fragmentations of life have become reconciled into a calming kind of unity.

What one weaves may be almost anything that calls for a decorative fabric. It may be as small as a pocket or as large as a room divider. However, I see no point in weaving what can be woven more quickly and efficiently by a ma-

8. A yoke in coarse white yarns with a medallion of silky bright colors by Annabelle Bergstrom.

9. *A pillow in green, blue and purple stripes by Helen Trescott.*

10. *A carrying poke with bead-trimmed fringe by Shelley Spring.*

16

11. A 4-hoop mobile to turn in the breeze by Bici Linklater.

12. A Christmas tree ornament woven in a pair of embroidery hoops by Pat Holtz.

17

13. *Pockets of burnt orange and green, with neck and sleeve braids to match, by Doris Fox.*

14. *A tiny bright circle to mark a sliding glass door by Beulah Rollyson.*

15. *A folding screen to hide the kitty-litter box, by Eunice Ewing. Millard, the Dendel rabbit, models.*

19

chine. If one is going to weave, why not weave original articles that do not come by the yard in fabric stores?

Most yardage, regardless of the weave, has the vertical threads at right angles to the horizontal. In needleweaving, one has the opportunity to interlace the threads in any direction. There is no need or reason to accept a boring machine limitation. By allowing the needle to roam at your whim in any direction, you become as free as a weaverbird, whose astonishing nests we would do well to study.

Gwen Frostic has stated this beautifully in her book, *A Walk with Me*. "Each bird has its own secret of nest building . . . but no bird has more than a bill to weave with . . . a foot to shape with . . . and its own body with which to mold the clay . . . and so with grasses, roots, twigs, bark, strings and mud they build their homes in which to raise their young . . . and line them with thistle, down, furs, mosses and feathers for comfort."

In our jingle, we list some of the things pictured in this book to tempt you. These projects are small in size, but big in imagination. Just as soon as you learn the basic weaves and knots (when you make your Tapestry Sampler—see Chapter 4), you will be ready to improvise and adapt designs for "unusuals" of your own.

16. *Handbag by Lois Renwick achieves textural interest by combining different yarns in a palette of many greens with sparks of bright red and yellow. Bag is lined with red silk.*

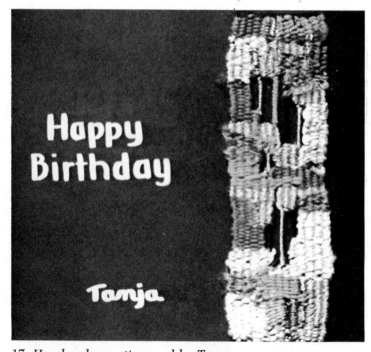

17. *Handmade greeting card by Tanya Baker. The mini-tapestry (3x8") attached to the card is handsome enough to frame.*

18. *You never reach the end or the all . . . Taurus woven over a shoe box—with one green eye, one blue—by Celia Wagner.*

*19. This metal hoop loom remains a permanent
frame for the weaving—warp is threaded through yarn
covering the ring. Frances Schroeder, weaver.*

3
Yarns, Looms and Needles

Needleweaving is not to be confused with stitchery or embroidery which are applied to a fabric that already has been woven. Weaving starts with a set of threads called warp, which are stretched, in our method, across cardboard or masonite. (Many kinds of looms have been developed over the centuries from a simple frame to complicated mechanisms—we are starting in the simplest possible way.) Weft is the thread that crosses and is woven into the warp. Because the more complicated looms may have a limiting effect on handwoven textiles, many present-day weavers have turned to the simple methods in order to gain freedom and flexibility in manipulating the yarns.

YARNS

First thing to do is collect a "library" of yarn in which to browse as you select the colors and textures you wish to use together. This need not be expensive. If you have friends who knit, probably they have baskets full of leftover odds and ends. Some yarn shops display sale prices on leftover single balls of yarn. You can unravel old sweaters and recycle them into your weaving. You can cut worn garments into strips, or you may be able to pick up scraps of fabric often available for nothing from upholstery shops to cut in strips; you may even want to unravel choice pieces for reweaving.

One outstanding weaver tells us he never begins a tapestry without collecting at least three textures of each of the colors he plans to use. If he has a texture he likes in white or in a light yarn, he will dye it to fit his color scheme, aiming not at a perfect color match but at something related to his scheme. If storage is a problem (and where isn't it?), fill a big salad bowl or a large basket with balls of yarn and use it as a color spot. An arrangement of yarn colors lifts the spirit and brightens the room.

For warp yarn, choose some kind that does not have much stretch. Carpet warp is a good cotton warp. Linen is excellent and in a four-cord twist is stronger than cotton carpet warp. Goat hair with a fuzzy texture gives an overall "bloom" to the finished work. My own preference is for dark warp. It gives a richness of color which one seldom achieves with white or light warp. You can see this in the illustration (Plate 21) where we have warped a cardboard half with light and half with a dark warp, using the same weft in both. In some cases you will want to use the same yarn for both warp and weft. But check yarn for both stretch and strength before you decide to use it for warp.

YOUR "LOOM"

Once you have yarns assembled, you need little else to begin. A cardboard or a piece of masonite slightly larger than the weaving will

Mobile
Pillow Dolls

Body
Stuffed
Weave front and
Back panels, add head
and arms after done

Head - a hoop.
Arms - woven
tassels at bottom.
Swing freely
Use beads —

20. To make a cardboard loom, cut slits ¼ inch deep and ¼ inch apart
in both top and bottom. There is enough margin space to note weaving
instructions for Beverly Nemetz's mobile dolls shown in Plate 5.

be your loom. For a small weaving, stiff cardboard is adequate. A larger cardboard loom should be reinforced on the back with a second piece of cardboard cut slightly smaller than the first one—this will keep it from becoming floppy as you work on it. Cut slits in the edge of the cardboard with scissors or an X-acto knife to a depth of about ¼ inch. Good spacing for the cuts is usually ¼ inch apart. For a rectangular weaving, you need make cuts only in the ends of the cardboard (Plate 20). For oval or circular forms, you need cuts all around.

For large projects, untempered masonite makes a more satisfactory loom than cardboard. It may be cut or notched with a handsaw or power saw. You'll find it helpful to paint the surface white. This makes it easier to see what you are doing as you weave.

Perhaps the simplest loom of all is to cut slits in both ends of a plastic meat tray—this makes an excellent loom for a child (Plate 22). The small oblongs he weaves on it can be sewed together to make a blanket for a doll.

When you finish a weaving you usually dispose of the loom. But sometimes you will want to work on a hoop which becomes the permanent frame for your design. It might be a metal hoop, a little heavier than coat hanger wire. Use the buttonhole stitch to cover the metal with yarn and run warp threads through this stitchery (Plate 19). Or use a wood embroidery hoop, notch or drill it to hold warp threads (Plate 4).

21. Detail showing the effect of light versus dark warp threads when the same weft yarns cross both.

22. A plastic meat tray is easy to notch for warping, makes an inexpensive practice loom for children.

*23. Ink the design onto the white background
of the cardboard loom before warping it.*

NEEDLE AND OTHER EQUIPMENT

A bent needle with a large eye is your first choice for needleweaving. If you cannot find a needle with a big eye which is also curved, you can curve it yourself with a pair of pliers. The needle will bend more easily if you heat it with a torch. Long bodkins are often handy, especially for plain weaves. You can make one: Drill a hole in one end of a long thin piece of brass; point the other end and bend it into a curve. You may find some Argyle sock bobbins useful, too, for carrying yarn.

You will need a tool for pushing the woven thread into place—technically called a beater.

A dog comb is good for this, or you may use any large toothed comb. Sometimes your fingers or the weaving needle will be all you need to compact the yarns—especially for irregular or loose weaving. It is desirable to reduce equipment to the bare essentials, so that you as a weaver may turn your entire attention to experiencing the character of the materials themselves.

Obviously, you will need a pair of scissors. And if you are following a definite design, a felt tip pen will be handy for blacking in the design on your loom (Plate 23).

4

Learning to Weave by Making a Tapestry Sampler

There are three good reasons for making a tapestry sampler. First, by completing it, you will learn all the necessary knots and weaves. Second, you will see and feel what the different textures look like—the effects you can get; this makes your sampler a valuable reference for future work. And third, chances are you'll own a new wall hanging! Most samplers are handsome examples of needleweaving art you will be proud to display in your home (Plate 24).

HOW TO WARP A LOOM FOR A SAMPLER

Cut a loom at least 12 by 18 inches from heavy cardboard. Cut slits on each end ¼ inch deep and ¼ inch apart.

Warp the loom with strong, non-stretchable thread (carpet warp or linen cord) using simple parallel warping, this way: Knot the end of the cord at the back of the loom, in the first slit near one corner. This knot simply holds the cord, keeps it from pulling out of the slit. Bring the warp across the face of the loom to the first slit in the opposite end, leading it to the back of the loom, then to the front again through the next slit. Continue leading the warp back and forth across the face of the loom, keeping warp in parallel rows and of even tension (Plate 25). Fasten warp in last slit with another knot at the back. (Note: The only warp thread that shows on the back of the cardboard loom will be the small stitch-like threads between the slits.)

If your yarn library holds rug yarn, this is a good inexpensive material to use for weft in a sampler, because it is large enough so you can see what you are doing.

24. Completed sampler of knots and weaves by Esther Dendel will become a decorative wall hanging when it is removed from the loom.

WINDING YARN

Wool is an elastic material and it should not be wrapped in tight balls—that takes the stretch out of it. Instead, wind yarn over two fingers as well as over the ball, to keep the winding loose. After a few turns, pull out the two fingers, place them elsewhere on the ball and again wrap over them. When I see a ball of yarn wound too tightly, I have an irresistible urge to rewind it, to liberate it!

THE WEAVER'S KNOT AND CHAIN STITCH

Cut the weaving yarn about two yards long to start; you will get a favorite length as you work. If it is too short, you waste too much time rethreading your needle. If too long, the weaving yarn gets worn as you drag it through the warp. Use longer lengths of tightly spun yarn, but shorter lengths of loose, easily frayed yarn.

Anchor the weft (weaving thread) to the warp with a weaver's knot (Drawing 26, Plate 27). (Note: The photo also shows another way to warp a loom, leading two strands of warp through each slit—this would permit additional texture variations.)

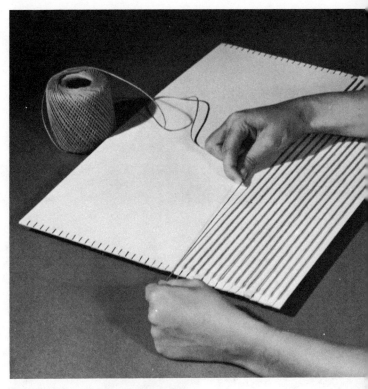

25. Cardboard loom has ¼" slits cut across top and bottom and is in the process of being warped.

27. Secure the weft to the warp with a weaver's knot.

26. Weaver's knot detail.

29

28. *Start to weave near the center of the loom—allow your needle to roam freely.*

29. *Before you begin a weaving, put in a row or two of chain stitch at both top and bottom of loom— to space warps evenly and hold them in place.*

30. *Chain stitch detail.*

Place the knot for your first stitches at one corner of the loom and do a few rows of chain stitch (Plate 29, Drawing 30). The useful chain stitch helps space the warps evenly and holds them in place—do a few rows at the other end of the sampler, too. You will also use the chain stitch in the body of weavings to outline shapes. You can chain over more than one warp.

Caution: It is important, in doing any of the stitches, not to pull the weft too tight. Keep your eye on the warps, especially at the selvages; if they're pulling out of line as you weave, loosen up!

After you have done the "securing" rows at both ends of the loom, move to the central area (Plate 28). I suggest this because I find my students get more spontaneous effects this way, as I do. You have a sense of freedom, allowing the needle to roam freely among the warps in the empty center area, making curves and loops. This is a great plus of needleweaving and it is a mistake not to take advantage of it.

THE PLAIN WEAVE

Try your first curve in plain weave (some call this the darning stitch). Take your needle over and under about a dozen warp threads; then turn around and come back under the warps you first went over, and over those you first went under (Drawing 31). Both rows should follow a simple arc. Continue adding rows to the arc, enlarging it by including an extra warp thread each time you turn. When you have done about 10 rows (or run out of thread), turn your loom around and weave a matching arc in mirror-image relationship to the first (Plate 32).

You now have an oval-shaped opening between the two arcs. This is a good place to change color. Fill the opening with more plain weave, over and under, around and around, until all the warps are covered (Plate 33).

THE EGYPTIAN KNOT

When the weft loops around the warp, the result is a knot-type of weave. To make the Egyptian knot, study Drawing 35 and Plates 34 and 36. See how the needle dips each time under two warps—the warp being wrapped and the next one to be wrapped. Practice the Egyptian knot by putting in three rows of it from edge to edge of the sampler, and following the curve of the central medallion (Plate 37).

The tricky part is turning around, reversing direction. When you get to the turn-around, look again at Plate 34. It shows how you wrap the outside warp twice; then dip under and around the next warp; then continue as before.

At first, it may be a little difficult to get the tension right when weaving Egyptian knots. It helps to hold one finger on the warp thread that is being encircled, pressing it in place as your other hand draws up the weft thread. When the Egyptian knot is well done, every wrap looks like a beautiful little bead of yarn. When several rows follow one another, they produce a rib in the direction of the warp.

31. The plain weave, easy as darning, is the basic stitch for needleweaving.

32. Start sampler with plain weave in several rows of a graceful curve—turn loom around and repeat motif.

33. Fill in the center of almond-shaped medallion by going around and around with plain weave.

34. Egyptian knot close-up showing how to turn around.

35. Egyptian knot detail.

36. Weaving Egyptian knot next to the medallion.

37. Weave three rows of the Egyptian knot across the sampler, following the curve of the medallion.

THE TAPESTRY SLIT

In ordinary weaving, the weft yarn crosses the entire expanse of warp. But if you bring a weft only part way across the face of the warp and then turn back, you are beginning the tapestry slit. If you weave up to the slit from the other side and again turn around, you are bringing the weaving forward on either side of the slit. *It is this slit which defines tapestry.* In olden days, this was the device used to change from one color to another, and much effort went into sewing up the slits when the tapestry came off the loom.

In contemporary tapestry, the slits are added for decorative effect, usually without a color change. We make them on purpose and leave them open.

Slits in tapestry must be planned. If they happen just once in a while, or singly, they will look more like moth holes than decorative texture. I have seen tapestries where the slits were so well placed that I found myself thinking of them as notes of music.

For this illustrative sampler, I planned seven slits above the medallion in my sampler. They are placed to repeat and echo the curve of the medallion. I used a ruler to space them, and marked the placement of each one with a line drawn on the cardboard loom. You should do the same.

When you weave these tapestry slits, use the plain weave (Drawing 38, Plate 39). Decorative weaves would detract from the texture you achieve with the slits. After the slits are woven and you are ready to cross the entire area again, you may see trouble. That's because the over-and-under sequence of the plain weave may vary from one area to another. I solved this problem by making a few rows of the Egyptian knot. Use it freely any time you run into difficulty in the sequence of the plain weave.

38. Tapestry slit detail.

39. Tapestry slit close-up shows weaving both sides of the slit at the same time—with two needles.

THE LOCKED SLIT AND THE DOVETAILED JOIN

You have filled much of the area above the medallion; now turn the loom around and work in the area below. Try weaving some simple shapes; I chose the shape of the capital letter "I", making three of them in the medallion color, using the plain weave (Plate 40). I also felt a design need to repeat the slits I used above the medallion, as you can see in Plate 24.

You can lock your shapes to the background with a single, interlocking tapestry slit (Drawing 41, Plate 42). Bend your two forefingers around each other to visualize this interlock. You may weave the shapes, and then weave up their sides with the background color, weaving each lock as you come to it. Or you may use two needles and bring the two colors forward at the same level. Instead of interlocking weft yarns, you could wrap each one around the same warp.

A variation on the locked slit is the dovetailed join (Plate 43) in which two or more rows of

40. Weave the I-shaped designs with plain weave.

weft are woven alternately around a common warp. The two colors meeting make a decorative serrated pattern.

SOUMAK LOOPING

If you have followed my sampler suggestions, you will have just a little space between the "I" shapes and the end of the loom, to fill with a couple of rows of Soumak looping. This is an Oriental stitch or knot, best described as being like the outline or stem stitch in embroidery, except you work it over warps instead of into woven fabric. You may go forward over two warps and back under one, or perhaps forward over four and back under two. You should alternate each row of Soumak loops with a row of plain weave; in this way, you will have all the loops going in the same direction (Drawing 44, Plate 45). Also the plain weave gives Soumak tapestry more durability and strength; this is especially necessary if you use Soumak for rugs.

Soumak can be made even more decorative. If you want a larger loop, work over a pencil which you pull out later. Or thread your needle with two different color yarns and use them as one—pink and red together, or blue and green.

THE GHIORDES KNOT

Another wrapped warp that will give you a lot of texture is the Ghiordes knot. Study Drawing 47, and Plate 46 to see how it is made; then practice a row of these knots above the slits in the top part of your sampler. You may cut the loops or leave them continuous; obviously, the fuzzy cut ends will provide more texture than loops. The Ghiordes knot is often used in rugs and is said to be named for an Anatolian village famous for rugmaking.

THE ALMOND MOTIF

While there are a few tapestry techniques yet to learn, you have mastered the basic ones, and

41. Lock-stitch detail—
use it where two colors meet
to avoid an open slit.

42. Lock-stitch close-up—used where
background meets I-shaped design.

43. Dovetailed join, where two or more rows
of background weft are woven alternately on
same warp as the outside edge of "I" motif.

44. Soumak looping detail—
alternate with a row of
plain weave for stability.

45. Soumak looping close-up, surrounded
by areas of plain weave.

46. Ghiordes knot—detail shows how to weave it and where to cut it to achieve a fuzzy texture.

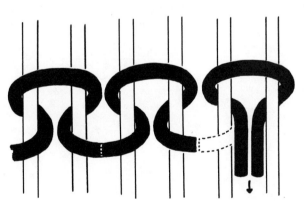

47. Ghiordes knot as used in sampler— after the three rows of Egyptian knots that closed the tops of the seven slits.

48. Almond motif close-up shows how you can push weft apart and weave in a new color.

49. French knots add textural interest
in areas that seem too flat.

only a little room remains on your sampler. Finish the space at the top with plain weave. When it is done, you might decide that you would enjoy a color change in certain spots. It's never too late! Just pull the weft apart, using both hands, some of it up, some of it down, to reveal bare warp in an almond shape. Thread your needle with a contrasting color and fill in these shapes with plain weave (Plate 48). The almond shapes are an excellent way to introduce darks into light areas and lights into dark areas. As you study the photographs in this book, you will see how many of our weavers employ the almond shape to break up space. If an area seems too large with nothing happening in it, you can always add almonds, even after every other part is finished.

REMOVING SAMPLER FROM LOOM

With a crochet hook, gently lift the loops out of the slits on the back of the loom. You can push the weaving out to occupy these little loops at the ends. Sometimes weavers tie fringe into the loops at the bottom of the tapestry. I did not do that, but the medallion needed more embellishment, so I added French knots (Plate 49).

5

After the Sampler...
Variations and Elaborations

Now that your own sampler is finished, you are ready to understand and enjoy the devices our weavers use in their work.

Study Jean Robinson's circular hanging which she wove on embroidery hoops instead of a cardboard loom (Plate 50, Color Plate 3). Inspired by a Tamayo painting, she chose soft colors: gold, rose, a muted earthy orange, green, turquoise, and then (it comes as a surprise) a touch of lavender. She warped the weaving on the smaller hoop, first with bands going in one direction. She planned her tapestry slits and did the weaving. Then she warped the bands going in the opposite direction through the tapestry slits in the first bands. The bands of weaving actually weave with each other. When the weaving was finished, Jean snapped the large hoop over the smaller one and tied the wrapped and twisted hanging yarns in place.

Notice that not all the slits were used for crossing warp. The open slit is in itself decorative. It does not have to do anything except *be* there. Jean worked for interesting divisions of

space, both in the bands and in the areas between the bands. As you think to yourself whether spaces seem interesting or dull, you will grow sensitive to design.

We show detail photographs from large weavings to give you a feeling for the design properties our weavers discover in the materials they choose and develop further by the techniques they use (Plates 51 and 52). Notice how their wefts meander freely, making curves and almonds; how they vary plain weave to show warp threads, compressing it or loosening it, adding knots and loops to get more texture. Do the wrapped warps intrigue you? You will find this device explained in Drawing 83.

Most tapestry experts seem to agree that the arrangement of light and dark areas is more important than the colors chosen for the work, and that the proportion of colors in relation to one another is most important. Usually fewer colors are used than appear in a painting. The emphasis is on changes of texture within a color —a number of whites of different weights in a

39

51. *Detail from a large weaving by Arvella Durham shows the effective texturing you can get by combining cut loops (Ghiordes knot), plain weave firmly woven, plain weave with warp showing, plain weave with several threads used as one, Egyptian knot and embroidered French knots.*

52. *Detail from Sharon Berg's weaving shows the variety of texture you get by changing the compactness of weaving. Much of the tactile beauty of tapestry is a revel in the threadiness of thread, the wooliness of yarn, the stubbornness of jute, the softness of silk.*

white area, a number of blues of different weights in a blue area, and so on. Very limited color schemes seem the most effective — three colors, or perhaps five being quite enough for one weaving, using several variations of tone in each color.

If the warp shows at all, and if it is dark, it has a harmonizing effect on whatever color scheme is chosen. Colors that might seem to clash or be too strident when placed side by side are often compatible with the neutralizing effect of a dark warp to harmonize them. Conversely, colors that seem pleasant together before they are woven often appear drab and dull or uninteresting after they are woven. The only way to determine what is good together is to try it; weave a sample of the colors you contemplate using.

50. *Circular wall hanging 20" in diameter by Jean Robinson. Bands with tapestry slits are woven directly onto wooden embroidery hoops which then become the permanent frame.*

53. Tapestry vest by Dr. Charles Stevens uses tapestry and staggered slits to expose a mauve lining behind the design done in several tones of green, from light to dark.

54. Staggered tapestry slit.

55. Variation of staggered tapestry slit. These slits can be made to have a stair-step effect by weaving over the warp more than once before moving the slit to a new position.

HATCHING

The method of moving from light to dark or from one color into another gradually is called hatching. Simple hatching is best understood by half-closing one's eyes and squinting at a printed column in a newspaper. The change of tone from solidly printed lines to lines that only partly cross the column is the principle involved in hatching.

In simple hatching, the lines of light yarn run parallel to the dark that they penetrate (Plate 57). In more complicated hatching, triangles of light color may be built up in the dark areas (Plates 58 and 59).

Almost everyone has favorite colors, colors to which he responds in a positive way. Starting with those colors you can gradually, through observation, extend the palette of your likes. Look at fabrics and objects in nature long enough to describe each color in words. The artist Van Gogh had remarkable skill not only in mixing colors in paint, but in observing color in nature and then describing it. We can read his published letters and know that when he looked at an old loom, he saw not just old wood but "greenish browned oak." His vision was precise. Our own becomes more precise as we work at making it so.

The most important thing about color is to enjoy it. Watch what happens when you weave a bright red yarn into orange or magenta warp. How different it looks when you change the warp to hot pink. Each color changes every other color, not only by weaving into the other but also by being near it. Watching these color changes and reacting to the change is an enjoyable way to extend your color sensitivity.

Dr. Charles Stevens produced an interesting effect by introducing a surprise color for the lining of his vest (Plate 53). You don't expect to see a low-key violet under the mossy green

56. Fur parka, tasseled feet, flapping arms are whimsical embellishments for stylized doll woven of white wool with brown symbol lock-stitched on its chest.

43

57. *Simple hatching, in which lines of one color of yarn run parallel to the color they penetrate to effect a color change.*

58. *Another example of hatching, more complicated, showing how triangles of colors are built up in block of another color.*

59. *Detail of an extremely intricate example of hatching, from Doris Fox's weaving (Plate 89).*

yarns. But when you see it, you are glad it is there.

A vest may seem quite a large undertaking to the beginning weaver, but it is actually very simple and easy to do. Dr. Stevens cut looms to match a vest pattern and warped them from top to bottom just the way you warped your sampler — the difference being that some of the warps end at the armholes. He used plain weave and tapestry slits; the open slits allow the mauve lining to show through.

Yarn in this weaving changes from one tone

of green to another in the pattern of points, repeated on vest back, too. This is done by weaving staggered tapestry slits (Drawings 54 and 55). You can stagger slits in each woven row as diagramed, or arrange them in stairsteps, as Dr. Stevens did; that is, by weaving not just one but several rows of weft before the slit moves to the new position.

In your sampler, you practiced locked slits, so you know how Beverly Nemetz wove the design into the body of her Eskimo Pillow Doll (Plate 56). The fur, the tassels, the design and the humor of the long, flat arms are interesting enough without adding complicated weaves or knots. Made to be hung as a mobile, the doll is done entirely with plain weave and locked slits. The head is a wrapped hoop, circled with fur.

Your sampler also taught you the Egyptian knot, which you will recognize as the rib in the background of the Virgo panel by Jo Dendel (Plate 60).

60. "Virgo" by Jo Dendel. One of 12 zodiac panels measuring 16" across top, 14" high. Egyptian knot gives background a ribbed effect; facial features are outlined with a couching stitch.

61. Detail of intricate laid-in design
used in a handwoven African blanket.
Collection of Mr. and Mrs. Jo Dendel.

6

More Techniques,
More Things to Make

A sampler is not quite big enough for you to learn all the useful tapestry techniques, so we suggest two more small projects: a pocket and a purse, both useful. The pocket is planned to give you confidence in doing a meandering weft. The purse will acquaint you with laid-in design.

MEANDERING WEFT

It takes more courage than most beginners have to start a large project with the weaving thread wandering at whim through the warps. But a little pocket, freely done, will show you how exciting this freedom can be. Rosita Montgomery started the pocket we picture without any sketch or any previous idea of what she might do. She simply selected some colors that would harmonize with a brown dress of coarse weave. Using the darkest weft, she ran it around through the warps (Plate 62), pushing it here, pulling it there, using the needle to slide the wefts somewhere else until the area seemed to be designed to please her. One can develop great sensitivity to design just by pushing a meandering weft around in an area, watching what happens, and reacting to it. If it "feels right", it probably is. The weaving continues, in freely meandering fashion, within the pre-

liminary outlines—a pleasing collection of textures and colors (Plates 63 and 64).

Instead of meandering freely, the weft thread may meander according to a plan. You can develop exciting texture if the weaving thread goes forward, turns back on itself for a space, turns and goes forward as before (Drawing 65, Plate 66).

LAID-IN DESIGN

A handsome and easy way to decorate plain weave is to add a contrasting yarn, laid in alongside the weaving thread. You may put the contrasting yarn in your needle along with the weaving thread and weave them in together. Or you may do the plain weaving first, darning in the contrasting color later. I wove a small purse with an orange rectangle on a field of green yarn; then came back to make a simple design of laid-in green yarn, following the ins and outs of the plain weave every fourth row in the orange rectangle. (Plate 67).

The five straight rows in the orange rectangle illustrate the simplest possible design using the laid-in device. African weavers make intricate and complicated use of it, as shown in the blanket we brought back from the West Coast of Africa (Plate 61).

47

62. Pocket loom 5x7" by Rosita Montgomery is warped with double strands of mohair yarn. The warp is separated by the two rows of chain stitch top and bottom so that in effect you have a loom warped ⅛" apart instead of ¼". Rosita weaves her design by using the darkest yarn first.

63. Finished pocket has the dark outlines filled in with a pleasing collection of colors and textures.

64. Pocket detail shows the variety of yarns and weaves used for fill-ins: plain weave, Egyptian knot, fine yarns, medium yarns and sometimes two colors in the needle at once.

48

65. *Detail showing a planned meandering weft.*

66. *Planned meandering weft as it looks on a loom—using double yarn (top) and single strand (below).*

I am so intrigued with the simplicity and the possibilities of laid-in design that I plan to explore it more deeply. For example, if one wishes to introduce beads into a weaving, this is a good way to do it (Plate 68). Simply string a bead on the contrasting thread each time it surfaces. When you weave the thread back under the warp, the bead is secured. Another idea: Make a knot in the contrasting thread each time it surfaces (Plate 69). This surface design of knots is a good starting point for future experiments.

THE ECCENTRIC WEFT

In tapestry from many parts of the world, we find weaving threads that are not at right angles to the warp. Rosita Montgomery wove a pocket

to experiment with this in a small way. When the unusual, or eccentric wefts as we call them, are quite noticeably eccentric and are tightly woven, small bulges appear on the surface. Because of this, the tapestry actually assumes a vaguely sculptured appearance. Tapestries from Egypt woven by the children of Harrania are a good example of this.

The picture we show (Plate 70) is a detail from a tapestry in the collection of Dr. and Mrs. William Wagner. The Wagners visited Harrania (a village near the Pyramids) and talked to Prof. Ramses Wissa Wassef, under whose direction the children work, weaving on simple wood frames. Nothing is drawn or designed in advance. The children simply create in a joyful, spontaneous way.

49

67. *Laid-in design: one row of background color is woven over every 4th row of color block. Ends of yarn are knotted for added decorative effect.*

Those who would like to read more about the project at Harrania will enjoy a book by the Forman brothers, they won the confidence of Professor Wassef and wrote a beautiful book: *Tapestries from Egypt.*

It is interesting that these glowing tapestries are now being woven within sight of the Pyramids in the very country where the ancient Copts wove the garments we study with close attention and gratitude today.

EARLY WEAVERS

The Copts were the early Christians of Egypt. We would know little about them had they not left a record of their culture in their graves. By the end of the third century most of Egypt had been Christianized. The Roman Empire was falling apart in the West. Out in the provinces and in monastic centers far from the great cities at the mouth of the Nile, the Copts de-

68. *Laid-in design of beads—as you weave over and under (plain weave) with contrasting yarn, add a bead each time needle surfaces.*

69. *Laid-in design of knots—same as for beads except you make a knot each time needle surfaces.*

veloped a truly individual and great art style. Many of their woven garments have influenced the vestments still in use in Christian churches today.

The Copts embalmed their dead. They dressed the body in linen and placed it on a wooden board with a pillow under the head, and buried it in the hot desert sands of Egypt. Spindles have been found in women's graves, weaving utensils and tools in men's graves. This division of labor—women spinning and men weaving—is the custom in much of West Africa today.

Making great use of Bible stories and the symbolism of their Christian religion, the Copts wove bands and medallions for their tunics. In their medallions, the amount of area to be filled determined the size of a figure; natural proportions gave way to design considerations. Perhaps that is why these compositions have an arresting charm. They surely do inspire contemporary weavers.

Discovering the Copts and the art they produced is just one of the serendipitous benefits of learning to weave, made all the more pleasurable because it is so unexpected.

An interest in weaving may also lead one deeply into the culture of our own Navajo Indians. Or into the lives and hearts of tribal Africa, as it did me. Peruvian tapestries from gravesites leave us incredulous; we get out a magnifying glass and try to understand their intricacies and technical skills. Some of these were made before the Spanish Conquest, even before the Incas came to southern and central Peru. We see vegetable colorings that glow after having been buried in the sands for two thousand years. We smell in the fibers the smoke from embalming fires lighted centuries ago.

One can travel back and forth through the centuries, and from continent to continent, making discoveries. And learning ever more about weaving.

70. Detail of a tapestry woven by children of Harrania, Egypt—
an excellent example of the eccentric weft used in freehand design.
Collection of Dr. and Mrs. William Wagner.

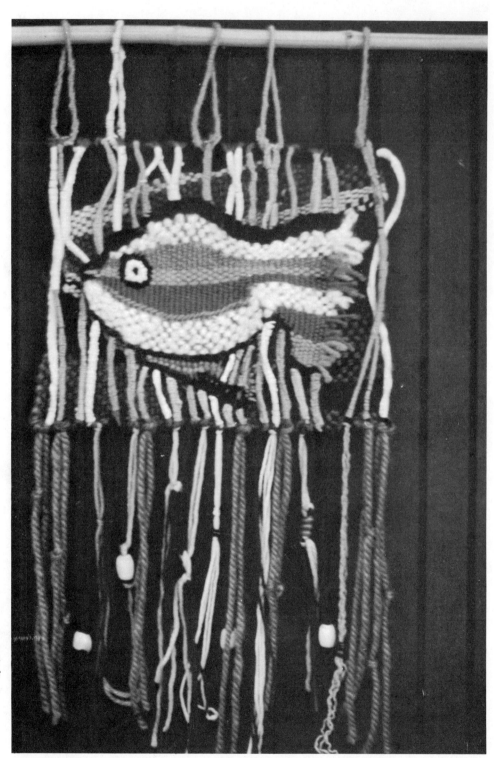

71. "Sun Fish" tapestry, 12x26", by Lisa Bannies. Woven on a loom that has been warped on both sides—fish is woven in front, waves in back.

7
Warping for Special Effects

So far we have been dealing with warps that lie parallel to one another and cover only the face of the loom. There are other ways to warp and some of them are very exciting. Suppose you want to make a seamless tube for a pillow or purse. You begin by cutting some hardboard for the project and notching both ends; these will be the top and bottom of your pillow or purse.

WARPING FRONT AND BACK OF LOOM

Our interesting problem is how to warp this without having the loom imprisoned in the finished work. The way out of weaving oneself into a corner is to warp the face of the loom just as you did for the sampler. Then turn the loom over and warp the back in the same way. The weft yarns go around and around the loom, front to back to front again, making a seamless tube. When the warps are lifted out of their notches on both ends of the loom, the loom slides right out the end. Do an oval shape the same way except be prepared to bend and break the cardboard to get it out of the opening, which will be smaller than the opening in a rectangle.

To get the effect of a two-level tapestry, you can warp both sides of the loom and weave them differently, instead of going around and around with the same pattern and weaving thread. In her little "Fish" tapestry, Lisa Bannies wove the back warp in a wave-like pattern to suggest the sea (Plate 71, Color Plate 5). The colors are ocean colors. On the front of the loom she wove the fish in the central area, and tightly wrapped the warps above and below the fish (see drawing 83). When she removed the loom, the ocean pattern behind the fish shows through the wrapped warps. Note that the side of the ocean on view is actually the wrong side of the fabric as it was woven on the back of the loom, so the weaver must be careful not to push any loose ends through to what seems to be the back but will really be the front of the work.

ECCENTRIC WARPING

We have talked about eccentric wefts and now we will see that warps can be eccentric, too, with interesting effects.

One begins an eccentric warp by crossing the central area of the loom instead of starting along one side. It follows a pattern: After leading the warp across the cardboard and through a slit to the back, you bring the second warp up through the slit to the *right* of the first warp. Then take it across the loom and down through the slit to the *left* of the starting warp. In other words, the warps cross on the face of the cardboard. Continue in this manner until the loom is warped. You'll have a considerable pile-up

72. *Dodecagon (12-sided) loom, 36″ across, by Jo Dendel—with weaving just started. Eccentric warps build up in center and are left exposed.*

where the warps cross; they are too close together to be woven, and need not be—they're interesting just the way they are. They give an extra dimension to the work. In Plate 72, you see how Jo Dendel warped a twelve-sided hardboard loom with the eccentric warp crossing the center.

But eccentric warp does not need to cross in the center. The work can be planned so that several of these warp build-ups take place in various areas of the loom. For ease of work, the bottom layer should be woven before the next layer of warp is strung out over it. See if you can find bottom among the warp crossings on Bici Linklater's loom (Plate 73).

Sometimes only part of a circle or rectangle is warped on the loom. Additional warps are anchored in the warp threads already on the loom and these take dynamic diagonal directions. You can see this in Jean Robinson's weav-

ing, which she calls "Winter." It is woven in Christmasy metallic threads (Plate 74).

WARPING SPECIAL SHAPES

If a weaving is not to be the same size on both edges, the difference can be managed by varying the spacing of the warp. Jo Dendel's loom in Plate 72 is sixteen inches along the top and ten inches at the bottom. The notches are of necessity closer together at the bottom. By starting at the center, one can usually adjust the difference by eye, but it could be mathematically calculated. The loom is warped with two threads in each notch in order to have extra threads with which to work in the parts of the design requiring detail (Plate 75).

Weaving collars and yokes presents this same problem of spacing the warp because the distance around the neck is less than the distance around the outer edge. In collars, the direction

54

73. "Crossing Paths", 14" square, by Bici Linklater. Eccentric warp runs diagonally from side to side as well as top to bottom. Strips are built up by weaving one layer before warping the next.
When finished, the weaving will be appliquéd on a pillow.

74. "Winter", 12" diameter, by Jean Robinson. Only scattered warp threads are attached to the wire circle—additional warps anchored to warps already there produce dynamic line movement within the circle.

of the warp changes with the structure. You can see (Plate 76) how Helen Hennessey marks a collar loom with ruled lines to show warp directions and spacing, prior to warping it. She worked it in rather fine yarns in a vivid blending of hot pinks, oranges and reds, with beads in the same colors (Plate 77, Color Plate 15).

You can form points by bringing the warps closer together toward the ends and also by weaving over two or more warps as though they were one. To make rays for a sun I wove, I warped a circular loom with eccentric warping, threads crossing in the center, and just

75. "Gemini" loom by Jo Dendel shows how to warp a trapezoid—there are the same number of slits top and bottom, but those at the bottom are closer together.

76. Cardboard loom (below) for collar has been ruled to show notching and to show direction and spacing for warp threads.

77. Finished collar (below, right) by Helen Hennessey is vibrant—Egyptian knots and laid-in beads are in purples, reds, pinks, oranges, greens and blues.

enough of them to get the width of the ray. Then I wove it from the outside edge to the center where the warps cross. The warp that continues on across the loom is not woven—instead, it's tied in a knot to make a tassel (Plate 78). When all the rays were woven, they were sewed to the perimeter of the sun.

Sometimes when a piece of work is to have considerable detail, one needs extra warps. The detailed area, a face for instance, can be woven on a separate small loom with twice as many warps as the larger area. The face in Plate 79 will be woven as sketched, removed from the cardboard and incorporated into a large tapestry. It is attached by pulling the warps of the large weaving, one at a time, through every other interval in the more densely warped piece.

Eva Fedorchek warped some correspondence cards with eccentric warp and the warp itself was so interesting that she did not need to weave into it. Each card is different as she rearranges the warping pattern (Plate 81).

Elizabeth Bennett wrapped three hoops of different sizes and fastened them together. The warps go in different directions in order to give variety to the finished weaving which will be done in bright colors (Plate 80).

Extra warps are often added and wrapped for textural effects. Plate 82 shows a band for a sleeve woven in white wool by Roméo Reyna. It is to be applied to a black dress. The added warps are long enough to twist and curl. They are secured by adding them to the warps in the woven area and weaving over both yarns as though they were one.

79. *Warping for face loom is half-spaced—closer weaving gives better detail. Woven face is then transferred to a larger tapestry.*

78. *Detail from wall hanging by Sharon Berg shows points formed by bringing warps closer at ends, weaving and then knotting them together.*

80. "Hoopla" by Elizabeth Bennett
is a wall decoration with three hoops—
warped in different directions. Weft
yarns will be in reds, pinks and oranges.

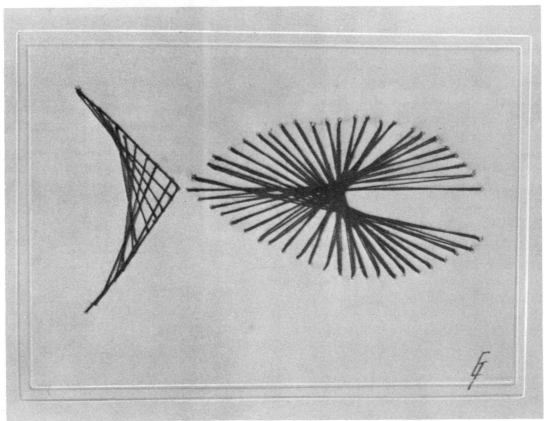

81. Correspondence cards with eccentric warping by
Eva Fedorchek are interesting with no further weaving.

THE YARN WRAPPING TECHNIQUE

Wrapped yarns give a distinctive effect, not otherwise obtainable. Wrapped yarns seem controlled, yet free. They are an easy way to introduce a Joseph's-coat-of-colors effect. Wrapping a thread makes it seem more important.

You may wrap warps simply by going around and around with a separate yarn. Catch the beginning of this yarn under the first few wrappings, and when you finish, work the end back under the wrapped area with a needle.

A somewhat easier way to secure the end of the wrapping yarn is to take a separate piece of yarn or thread and form a loop. Use the loop to anchor the wrapping yarn (Drawing 83). You may use thread of a different color for this —it is easier to find and pull out when its job is done. Run the loop from the bottom of the area to be wrapped to a point a little above where you want to stop wrapping. Wrap both warp and loop together, around and around up to the loop. Thread the end of the wrapping thread through the loop and pull it down into the body of the wrapped area by pulling the two ends of the loop from the bottom. Snip off the pulling ends of the thread close to the wrapping, or pull the thread out. We learned this technique from fishermen who use wrapping to prepare their gear.

82. *Sleeve band by Roméo Reyna has added warps that have been wrapped to give them more importance.*

83. *Detail of wrapping technique—to secure end of wrapping yarn, form a loop of contrasting thread and wrap yarn as shown, then pull yarn end into wrapped area.*

84. *Collection of mandalas shows the many interpretations artists*
give to the symbol of the sun. Woven by Frances Schroeder,
Jean Robinson, Helen Dickey, Helen Trescott, Louanne Matsler.

8
Weaving a Mandala

The sun, which "like a strong man runs its course with joy", is probably the inspiration for more great design than any other natural object. Sometimes circular designs represent the actual sun. At other times, a circle may be a symbol of the earth, the full moon, a bird's nest, eternity. Carl G. Jung, the famous Swiss psychologist, called our attention to *mandala*, a Sanskrit word meaning a magic circle.

Dr. Jung saw the mandala as a symbol of the harmonious relationship of a man with his Self. In his book, *Man and His Symbols*, he notes many examples from many cultures. He shows us a Navajo sand painter making a mandala in a ritual healing. After the patient has circled the mandala, he must sit inside it. In far-separated cultures, people contemplate a mandala to restore wholeness of the spirit and to achieve inner harmony.

Someone has pointed out that when children play joyful, peaceful games, they form themselves into a mandala. There are the singing games done in a circle, the Maypole dance,

many folk dances. Aggressive games such as "Crack the Whip" are more likely to take the form of a straight line.

Mandalas appear in children's drawings from all over the world, and if a child is left to himself without guidance about what he shall draw, he will sooner or later come up with a mandala. This, then, must be a symbol of universal attraction. It has been said that man does not invent symbols; he *discovers* them. The search to discover leads to interesting patterns of thought and to art that has more than surface meaning.

One of the best ways to contemplate a mandala is to weave one. Sometimes the weaving is done on cardboard and then transferred to a wire ring or an embroidery hoop; sometimes the hoop or ring is wrapped with yarn and the warping and weaving is done directly inside the circle. We have gathered some of the mandalas done by our group of weavers to show the variety possible within the confines of a circle (Plate 84, Color Plate 1).

85. *Nine mandalas woven by Judy Whelan for a walnut screen designed by Jo Dendel. Designs are unified by using the same colors for all.*

Jean Robinson wove a mandala for each of the four seasons. *Autumn* is a circle bound by braided cornhusks and done in the colors of turning leaves. *Winter* is in Christmas gold. *Spring* is as delicate as new leaves and fresh shoots of bulbs and grass. *Summer* looks as hearty as a vegetable harvest—the greens of peppers and peas, the reds of ripe tomatoes. As the seasons wheel into time, she takes the appropriate mandala out of storage and hangs it to mark the event.

Nine mandalas woven by Judy Whelan on 18-inch wire hoops were set into walnut frames, to make a folding screen for her husband's of-

fice. The screen itself was designed and made by Jo Dendel (Plate 85, Color Plate 11). The same vivid wool colors run through all of the mandalas, but each one is a unique expression of the weaver's skill and imagination.

Virginia Weeks' oval-shaped mandala was woven on notched oval cardboard. She positioned the finished weaving, still on its loom, inside a large wooden hoop and anchored it to the hoop with yarn laced through the mandala's warping loops, then removed the cardboard (Plate 86, Color Plate 8). The same device, but with entirely different effect, was used by Louella Ballerino (Plate 87, Color Plate

86. Oval mandala by Virginia Weeks is warped into a round ring with yarn—no further weaving. Beads are added to the fringe for interest.

87. Round mandala by Louella Ballerino, warped and woven in an open cross and square pattern, is set into a larger ring with radiant warping. Rays are woven, and gossamer threads strung with beads are tied here and there.

88. Detail showing how a mandala is warped to the loom for the second stage—weaving around it. Warp is threaded into the loops before the mandala is removed from its own cardboard loom.

7). Virginia's weaving is solid, textured with coarse yarn; Louella's is as ethereal as gossamer beaded with raindrops. Both are delightful.

A mandala may be thought of and hung as a completed weaving. Or it may become the focal point and center of interest of a larger creation.

Why not weave the mandala into a larger tapestry in the first place, instead of transferring it from a small cardboard to a larger loom? This is often done. But there are at least two advantages in making the small weavings first and later doing something further with them. First, this gives the weaver a beginning, something to work around. There is something rather frightening about a large blank set of warps. It is a little like a blank sheet of white paper that a writer knows he must fill. Writing anything, just anything, to get rid of the appalling blankness of that rectangle of paper is a help. The small weavings, set into the warps of a big loom, help you get started.

The second advantage of weaving these centers of interest first is that the warp in the small weavings may go "any which way" (eccentric warping), giving additional design interest.

The first step in bringing the small mandala into a larger weaving is to decide on the size of the larger statement and prepare a cardboard or piece of masonite with notches to receive the warp. Before beginning to warp, it is a good idea to place this loom on a table top where you will walk by it several times a day. Arrange the small weaving or weavings (still on their looms) where they seem right to you. Each time you pass the arrangement you have made, study the position of the mandalas. Move them a little this way or that. React to the new positionings. The most satisfactory designs come about if you, the designer, have been willing to indulge your inborn passion for arranging. When the locations feel right to you, mark their positions on the loom.

Begin warping as you did for your sampler. When you come to one of the mandalas, thread the free end of the warp through a needle, bring it into the back of the mandala's cardboard circle, threading it through the little stitch-like showings of warp (Drawing 88). Sometimes you will not know which loop of warp to secure, but it does not matter very much so long as the warps on the larger loom keep running close

89. Wall hanging by Doris Fox shows how the mandala blends into a larger weaving in waves of color using the hatching technique (Chapter 5).

64

1. Mandalas by
Frances Schroeder
Jean Robinson
Helen Dickey
Helen Trescott
Louanne Matsler

2. "The King"
by Esther Dendel
18x45"

3. Mandala
by Jean Robinson
20" diameter

4. "Pink Rock"
by Louella Ballerino
12x20"

5. "Sun Fish"
by Lisa Bannies
12x26"

6. *"Jubilee" and
detail of turkey-bone fringe
by Tess Goldsmith
11x30"*

7. *Mandala
by Louella Ballerino
14" diameter*

9. Tablemat
by Esther Dendel
13x19"

10. "Rising Sun"
and detail of slit weave
by Roméo Reyna
4½x8'

8. Mandala
by Virginia Weeks
15" diameter

11. *Mandala Screen*
by Judy Whelan
frame by Jo Dendel
each square 22"

12. "Off and Away"
by Helen Hennessey
22x36"

13. Hoop Tapestry
by Tess Goldsmith
4x6'

14. Woven necklace
by Annabelle Bergstrom

17. *Dress and mandala trim detail by Rosita Montgomery*

15. *Purple neckpiece by Helen Hennessey*

16. *Red-red belt by Judy Whelan 40" long*

90. *Variation on pillow design #92 shows repeat of elements to make a rectangular tapestry.*

92. *Tapestry appliqué for a pillow top by Jean Stange shows design plan, finished mandala and cardboard looms with work in progress.*

91. *In another variation the mandalas are repeated in clusters, in small, medium and large sizes.*

to parallel, one with the next. If a long length of warp tends to snarl, do not hesitate to cut it to a convenient length and then tie a knot in it when you have need for more. The knot will be embedded in the finished weaving and will not show. Some notches on each side of the circle will not be used at all, but this does not matter; the weft threads will weave into and secure these. Remove cardboard from mandala after warp from the larger panel comes into the warp of the mandala.

After ensnaring the principal design area or areas (the mandalas) into the total area, the next design problem is to draw some lines that will relate these shapes into a total compo-

93. *Award-winning tapestry by Tess Goldsmith combines mandalas with intertwined woven strips and fringe in a fantastically complicated weaving that started with three embroidery hoops.*

sition. Our group felt that Doris Fox was unusually successful in solving this problem (Plate 89). Her weaving is in mossy greens, burnt oranges, browns and white. As she moved from one color to the next, she used the tapestry device known as *hatching*.

Jean Stange grouped one mandala shape with three linear shapes of varying widths. These were woven, each on its own loom, then the shapes were sewed to textured neutral linen to make a pillow top (Plate 92). Jean later thought of using the same looms to repeat the design in other colors for the opposite side of the pillow.

Next, her explorations led to the use of three mandala shapes, each a different size, combined with lines that utilize the total area of a large rectangular weaving. Subtleties of shading and color changes will be worked out on the loom. Experience shows that tapestries that hold to-

94. *Individual squares from the screen in Plate 85 used as wall decoration—a good solution if you like the idea of walnut-framed mandalas but you have no use for a screen.*

gether visually, from a design standpoint, have some large sweeping lines that cross most of the area (Drawing 90).

Jean's third experiment led to the clustering of mandala shapes, again of varying sizes (Drawing 91). If a shape is repeated, or nearly repeated, in small, medium and large proportions, it sets up a rhythm—a progression of size intervals. Having all the shapes in a composition the same size is a little like music written entirely in whole notes. The monotony of such a song may be soothing, but soon we are lulled to sleep, or we're longing for some excitement —a change of pace.

Another thing we experience in Jean's designs is the satisfaction of the bent line. A bent line is a curve that is straight for part of its length. It is a good design line because it combines the grace of the curve with the strength of a straight line. It is particularly good in these three designs because the designer employs it to reconcile the curves of the mandalas to the rectangles of the tapestries.

To see how an artist develops a complex tapestry, look at Tess Goldsmith's hanging that grew from three embroidery hoops (Plate 93, Color Plate 13). She wrapped the three hoops, each a different size, and warped and wove each one differently. She then warped a large frame with dark warp and distributed the hoops within the area. Since the weaving would be quite large, more circles seemed necessary. These were woven and added. Slender woven strips came next, playfully interweaving with other woven strips. Finally, the entire warp expanse was brought together, woven with triangular color transitions at the bottom of the hanging. The colors are rich reds, pinks, mustards and golds. This hanging is an award-winning tapestry. As one approaches it, the awesome overall effect gives way to a desire in the beholder to examine each intricacy, each texture, each wrapping of yarn.

68

95. A desert stone inspired this small tapestry by Louella Ballerino. Extra yarns are tied into warp to make the long fringe (Chapter 10).

9

Where Design Ideas
Come From

If, as you worked on your sampler, you found pleasure in manipulating the yarn, if you felt a tingle of exultation, no matter how faint, you've known the first stir of something that may become very important to you. It may completely change your life.

That great thinker, Martin Buber, has told us that we may treat things, other persons, and even ourselves, either as an "it" or as a "Thou". A Thou feeling of respect toward the universe is the hallmark of the craftsman. This does not mean that he "just loves everything". In fact, he is highly discriminating. He can have Thou feelings only toward that which is honestly itself. He cannot relate to the tawdry, the sham or the show-off. Elegance is sometimes an offense. The thread from an old potato sack may have more appeal for him than cords that glitter and shine. It is more earthy and closer to its source.

We have in our time become alienated from the earth. Jute, wool and sisal, puffs of unbleached cotton, driftwood and shells and peb-

bles, sea-polished glass and bleached bones, a seed pod, a weathered barn board, a bright feather dropped from a bird in flight—these are a few of the offerings from earth. We are free to ignore or accept. But we need to cultivate a friendship with earth and what it offers.

When I was a child growing up on an Iowa farm, I did not think old potato sacks or unpainted barn boards or milkweed pods were beautiful. My mother said they were, but I thought she was just clutching at something to be glad about; that was her nature. To me, the potato sacks suggested back-breaking stoop labor in the fields. Weed pods were from plants that should have been hoed out before they set seed. Unpainted barn boards were a constant reminder that money was short and that shoes for school in the fall after a barefoot summer were more important than paint for the barn.

It was only when I came back to these familiar things after having lived with the tribespeople of West Africa who revere the earth as their Great Mother, that I realized what my

96. Photograph of dried salt and mud forms suggests design lines and colors for a weaving.

97. Weaving in process: In a free translation of her photograph, Joan Coverdale improvises with yarn textures and colors—even with seaweed.

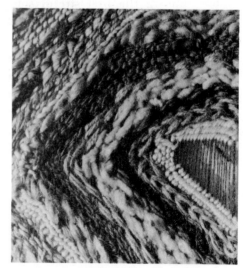

98. Detail showing how variations in color, yarn texture and weave interpret dried salt and mud forms.

99. *Heavily textured weaving by Phil Freeman employs the symbols of Cross and circle. Red and orange yarns are used together in loops for intense color effect. Weights at bottom are stoneware medallions.*

100. *Freely but also intricately woven Cross by Jean Freeman stands 4½ feet tall. Both warps and wefts meander freely, crossing every which way. Colors are appropriate to an adobe church: purples, reds, greens and white. The four crossed sticks were pushed through warping loops (but not through all of them) when the weaving was finished.*

own mother had been wise enough to know all the time. Perhaps my friendship and feeling for these earth things is firmer and deeper because I came back to it from half the world away. And this is why sticks and stones and bones find their way into my work.

DESIGNS IN NATURE

Sometimes a certain stone is not physically attached or embedded in a tapestry but the contemplation of the stone suggests the color and design of the tapestry. A stone picked up in a California desert provided Louella Ballerino with all the impetus she needed to do a splendid little tapestry. She did not try to copy the stone, but to interpret it (Plate 95, Color Plate 4).

What next? A walk on the beach or along a meandering stream. A time of browsing through meadows and woods. Chase some shadows as they change with the breeze and the light. Study the pattern of bark on a tree, the whirl of eddying water in a pool.

PHOTOGRAPHS

Color photography has relieved the artist of the need to show how things actually look. The artist's new duty is to help us know the feeling aroused by a beautiful object in nature. A tapestry does not need to represent precisely any scene or object. It may come closer to nature if it does not. One design device which many

101. Zodiac signs by Jo Dendel. Background will be done in Egyptian knot, circular designs in plain weave outlined with the couching stitch.

102. Couching stitch: detail shows how masonite is drilled following circular line so a couching thread can be wrapped from back of loom around warp and laid-on yarn. The laid-on yarn defines the circle, separates it from background.

73

103. Child's drawing duplicated in weaving by Celia Wagner on a loom warped horizontally. White halo effect around the figure is a device the weaver admired in a Polish tapestry.

104. Polish tapestry detail (from the Allen-Related Art Dept. collection owned by the University of Wisconsin) shows figure separated from background by halo effect.

105. Like many weavers, Helen Dickey uses yarns to enmesh and display found things. Here she has subordinated the yarns to emphasize the twigs.

artists find useful is to project slides of scenes they have photographed. Turn them out of focus until the literal subject matter disappears and only the colors and shapes, the dark and light patternings remain. Photographs of autumn color, of ocean tide pools, of sunsets and many other natural beauties lend themselves to this treatment. This is a sort of distillation of the poetry in scenes that have moved us.

Joan Coverdale is interested in the sea life and birds of our Newport Bay. She photographed an area that she calls "Dried Salt and Mud Forms" (Plate 96). Not as a copy of her photograph, but using it as an inspiration, she repeated some of the shapes and shadings in her tapestry (Plates 97 and 98). The tapestry is in the colors of salt and sand and she has used some seaweed in the weaving along with jute and yarn. Seaweed gets very stiff and unwieldy when it is dry but if it is left out in the dew overnight, it becomes pliable again and can be threaded in a needle.

SYMBOLS

Symbols produce in us feelings and moods that bypass language; indeed, symbols have no need of words. At the time the great cathedrals were built in Europe, Christian symbolism was a language which even the illiterate understood. In secular as well as in religious life, bright banners were everywhere. Flags waved at jousts and fluttered from gay tents. Knights had their own colors and during the Crusades, they carried the symbol of the Cross to faraway lands.

The bright red tapestry by Phil Freeman with its symbols of Cross and circle (Plate 99), seems to have come right out of those vigorous times. The stately medallions of stone he used for weights on the bottom echo the theme of the weaving. The entire effect is achieved through change of textures in the red and orange yarns which in the loops are used together as one.

106. A white tapestry on brown warps by Helen Hennessey traces the curves of two tree branches. After weaving, warps from rectangular loom were pulled through holes drilled in branches. The weaving is an outstanding example of improvisation within the boundaries of the branches.

107. *Tearing up paper and arranging it often suggests a design idea. To Mr. and Mrs. Roger Dunn these shapes looked like the Rocky Mountains as seen from a jet plane. They paper-clipped torn papers to warps and have started to outline them for a 4x6' wall hanging that will be worked in mountain colors.*

The Cross, woven by Jean Freeman and mounted on four crossed sticks, is in purples and reds and greens and white. It seems to belong in an adobe church in the American southwest and would add warmth as well as meaning to the wall (Plate 100). The rough textures, the vivid color, the spontaneous, almost unfinished appearance of the weaving give it a force and directness which are lacking in many smoother and more painstaking pieces of work.

The Star of David, the Menorah, the Christian Cross, all provide the designer with ideas for beautiful hangings for temple or church.

SIGNS

Some people take astrology seriously and some only dabble at it, but almost everyone at least knows what his own sign is. The signs of the zodiac are a design challenge because it is difficult to combine in the same composition subjects as different as a bull and a virgin. Jo Dendel found that composing each sign within a circular form gave a unity to the disparate subject matter (Plate 101). In the weaving, the same colors will be used in each unit, giving further unity. The round design motifs will be in plain weave, the trapezoid background in Egyptian knot rib weave.

It was felt that the circle enclosing each motif should be really round, not wobbly. In order to weave it so, Jo drilled holes close together in the masonite loom and couched a thread around these outlines. The couching is done over the top of the warp and holds it exactly in place (Drawing 102). While couching is an embroidery device, it lends itself in weaving to making the warp more manageable. The finished units (see Plate 101) will hang in two vertical groups, six signs in each group.

CHILDREN'S DRAWINGS

Children make delightful drawings which all too often are tossed in the wastebasket because mothers do not always appreciate the direct, spontaneous quality of what children do. To transpose a child's drawing into some more permanent medium is a way to dignify what he has done. Celia Wagner's tapestry copies a drawing by a child without tampering with it in any way. We see a horse with legs like wet noodles and a tail that has slipped from

108. *Experienced weavers like Helen Hennessey may start working on a loom without any design in mind, improvising as they go, weaving a small unit first and building on it. She calls this tapestry "Off and Away", which describes her blithe approach. Plate 120 shows fringe detail.*

109. *Inspired by her materials, Sharon Berg lets a few weft threads hang loose at sides of "Navajo Textures" wall hanging, to show the yarn in its natural state. Pieces of driftwood are used for accent. Plate 78 shows in detail how the points at bottom of tapestry are woven.*

where tails ought to be. This is precisely part of the charm of the design and any "improving" by an adult would be sure to ruin it (Plate 103).

The technique of using a white halo effect beyond the black outline of the drawing was suggested by studying a Polish tapestry owned by the University of Wisconsin (Plate 104).

WEAVING TO DISPLAY TWIGS AND THINGS

Weavers, so responsive to the earth's friendship offerings, can't bear to waste even a twig. And they find in weaving a way to enmesh the special twigs or sticks that come their way, too interesting to throw away. In Helen Dickey's

110. Fine red threads remain hidden in "Puff of Blue" knotted in Annabelle Bergstrom's hanging, until the close observer yields to his impulse to touch it. The surprise is quite in character with the spontaneity shown in the weaving.

111. Beginning somewhere in the middle of her loom with a meandering needle, Celia Wagner evolved a boldly creative design in texture and oblique line to make this heavily fringed purse.

weaving, the thread is almost secondary in interest to the sticks she wants to display (Plate 105). Roméo Reyna's hanging began with twigs he pruned from a bush (Plate 113).

TORN PAPER DESIGNS

One of the most effective ways to design for weaving is to tear newspaper quickly into shapes. Look at each shape as you tear it. Do you tend to tear little shapes all the same size? Work at varying the sizes. Are they all similar in shape? Try notching into the edges with more careful tearing. Pierce some of the shapes by tearing holes in the interior areas. These shapes need not look like anything in nature, but some of them accidentally will. You may have started without any idea of what you wanted to do, but the shapes you tear or the shapes the torn paper makes as you assemble them may suggest your subject.

The light shapes you see in Plate 107 were torn first. No definite subject matter was in mind; in fact, several persons made a game of tearing up paper. When the papers were arranged to form some continuity over the entire area, they suggested the land patterns one sees when flying over the Rocky Mountains in a jet after some of the snow has melted, leaving the dark rocks and earth exposed on the tops of the ridges. Dark areas were then torn to support the idea. The torn paper was pinned to the warp to be used as a guide in the weaving. In the photo, the dark shapes have already been outlined with meandering (eccentric) weft and the paper removed. The colors in this particular tapestry are the blues of great expanses of clear, clean air, the whites of snow and fog and mist, the yellow greens of lichen, the forest greens of conifers, the blacks and browns of rock and earth, the purples of distant haze. The tapestry is large (4x6 feet) and is being woven by Mr. and Mrs. Roger Dunn for a particular blank space between clerestory windows in their living room. Because of the large size, the tapestry is warped on a frame of hardwood rather than on masonite. The frame will be removed when the weaving is finished.

Mike Hudson started with a lion in mind, tearing up colored construction paper to design his lion pillow (Plate 2).

112. *Improvising a piece at a time on irregularly shaped looms, Winifred Roth decides later what they'll be. Her tapestry sculpture, the pieces sewed together over a wire form, combines soft blues and neutrals with black horsehair.*

IMPROVISATION

Weavers who have done several tapestries, and once in a while a real beginner, can start on a loom without any preconceived idea, weave a small unit and build upon that. Helen Hennessey works almost entirely in this way. Each area she weaves makes a happening that seems to call for other happenings around it. To improvise without even a beginning sketch is perhaps the most free and creative of all ways to work. It takes a certain boldness of mind, an innovative attitude and a willingness to fail if need be. It is like starting a journey without having any idea of destination and this requires a daring spirit and courage. Of course, if what one does is not working, one can always take it out. What that requires is the dedication of a true craftsman.

"Off and Away" by Helen Hennessey is a tapestry done in coarse white textured yarns, dark blues and purples in several weights and many tones of aqua in the background area. Plain and rib weaves mix at will and the weft is seldom at right angles to the warp except in the beginning and ending of the work. It seems to me an almost perfect example of what a good tapestry should be (Plate 108, Color 12).

Another tapestry by Helen Hennessey combines many tones of white and near-white yarns woven into brown warps that protrude in a decorative way through two bent tree branches (Plate 106). The first rows of the weaving at either end of the tapestry follow the curves of the sticks; these curves were drawn on the cardboard loom as a guide. Wrapped warps form negative shapes through which the color of the wall behind the tapestry will show.

Another weaving which "just grew" is the purse by Celia Wagner (Plate 111). It is difficult to start any motion, difficult to get any forms to "start growing" unless one *begins weaving in the central area of the warp.* The very first line of weaving may be pushed about this way and that, to establish the boundary of a form for beginning oblique movements of the weaving thread (eccentric weft).

Annabelle Bergstrom's hanging, "Puff of Blue", started with a puff of dark blue tufted knots in a field of light, heavily textured yarns

113. Between twigs (prunings from a bush on his property), Roméo Reyna stretches a sampler's variety of weaving techniques.

(Plate 110). You want to touch the woolen sheen of the knotted area and when you do, you are rewarded by the sight of fine red threads hidden among the roots of the knots. The weaver is saying in a subtle way, "Please *do* touch." The reward is more than the feel of the yarn under the fingers; there is the bonus and the surprise of the fine rich red threads which no one sees except he who looks deeply.

Winifred Roth is another weaver who starts without any notion of the finished product. Often she cuts irregular looms and after the weavings are finished and off the loom, she decides how to combine them. Sometimes she sews them together over a frame of bent wire soldered into sculptural form. Subtle variations of neutral colors and a soft blue are combined with black horsehair and coarse Mexican yarns in her tapestry sculpture (Plate 112). It has the force and mystery of the costumes and masks worn in Africa by tribal shamans.

Sharon Berg starts her weavings by contemplating the textures of coarse Navajo yarns, some of them so slightly spun they are almost fleece. By allowing the ends of some of the weft threads to hang down in a sort of bouquet at the sides of the weaving, she permits the full beauty of the yarn in its natural state to be enjoyed. Sometimes she breaks up a large area by adding warps and weaving strips that lie on top of the background color. None of these devices is planned before she begins weaving (Plate 109).

This extraneous approach turns up many surprises. It guarantees that every tapestry is one-of-a-kind. The weaver could not, and would not, copy even her own work. It is a contemporary way to work, in sharp contrast to the old custom of artist-drawn cartoons faithfully copied by artisans who patiently matched the colors of their yarns to the artists' paints.

114. This 4x6' wall hanging by Roméo Reyna incorporates a mandala done in tones of blues, browns, and whites (including tufts of fur).

DESIGN IN EVERYDAY LIFE

If you were to visit the home of Roméo Reyna in Laguna Beach, California, you would find great masses of flowers blooming in unglazed stoneware pots made by the artist. The blaze of color that meets your eye comes from hundreds of fuschias, gardenias, begonias and succulents. You would be wrapped in sound from the aviary, where more than seventy finches and canaries and other exotic birds sing and nest and preen their brilliant plumage.

83

115. "Setting Sun" by Roméo Reyna is a 5x7' wall hanging with a bright red mandala woven into a dark background. Generous use of the tapestry slit gives the sun a shimmery texture.

Inside the Spanish-type house, you would find a 17th Century altar and shelves filled with pre-Columbian art. The kitchen is a place to linger and look and smell. A delicate aroma comes from a wreath of braided herbs even when nothing is cooking on the stove set above bright Mexican tile. Everywhere throughout the house you will find balls of bright yarn. It is arranged in baskets, even hung from the ceiling in wire containers. But to see Roméo's weavings in process you will need to go out to the patio because many of the works are too large to be woven indoors. (Color Plate 10.)

One weaving was done by trimming and warp-

ing the branches of a dried Christmas tree. Another weaving was done directly into a wooden hoop three feet across, with fringe 60 inches long. Roméo likes the yarn spun by our American Indians, and mohair, cow hair, rope and silk. All his weaving is done with a needle and most of it is in plain weave. The effects come, not from fancy knots but from the textures of the yarns and the juxtaposition of glowing colors. And almost always, his motif is a mandala (Plates 114 and 115). These weavings find their way into homes and offices, into art shows and museums across the nation and abroad.

Roméo has trained at three art schools, but his inspiration comes from the simple land of his childhood. As a small boy, he swam in the Rio Grande and brought clay from the river bank to his Mexican grandmother who showed him how to form it into animal shapes which they fired in the ashes under the huge outdoor laundry kettle. These were the beginnings of a sophisticated artist who has successfully bridged two cultures, two worlds and is at home in both.

It is largely due to the encouragement and Roméo's generous sharing of ideas that our own craft group became so totally engrossed in needlewoven tapestry. For many of us, tapestry making has become almost a way of life.

We have digressed for a few paragraphs to say something about Roméo's life-style because we believe that the environment of an artist, the way he sets the table and cooks his food, the objects with which he surrounds himself are all in some subtle way involved with what he has to say in his work. They are just *there* without anyone knowing how they got there. The clay of the Rio Grande, the strings of Ruby red peppers hung against the walls of adobe houses, the colorful patterns of the markets of Mexico, the potato sacks of the harvest fields —all these have been distilled, and it is the essence of these things and many more that make the beauty and the poetry of Roméo's weaving.

10

Finishing and Hanging the Weaving

When you finish your sampler or other tapestry and it's ready to hang, lift the loops of warp out of the slits on your loom with a crochet hook. Poke any ends of yarn to the back side and weave them into the body of the weaving before snipping them off.

Some tapestries look better with a concealed hanger. When it was decided that a fringe or wrapped sets of warp would detract from Christine Cooke's tree tapestry (Plate 116), she stitched a flat, thin stick to the back (Plate 117). The stick stretches and holds the weaving to its full width as well as providing a way to hang the work. Your sampler could be hung this way.

Tess Goldsmith's tapestry is more informal in design and a purplish twig pushed through the loops of warp at the top seemed just the right hanger (Plate 119, Color Plate 6). This tapestry is weighted at the bottom with bones from a turkey neck which were bleached and then dyed with red onion skins. A few smaller neck bones are strung like beads and incorporated into the body of the weaving.

An informal bent branch seemed to fit with Jean Robinson's little weaving of a tide pool (Plate 118). Wrapped warp added at the top of the weaving gives it a larger dimension.

Wrapped warp leads to stoneware beads which weight the bottom.

Along the bottom edge of her weaving, Helen Hennessey uses a row of blue beads made of Egyptian paste, wrapping the warp below the beads instead of above them. The warp is blue and the wrapping yellow green (Plate 120).

The top of this same weaving is a polished mahogany bar drilled with holes. Each group of warps is pulled up against the bottom of the bar of wood with a cord from top (Plate 121).

To make fringe to extend the size of her tapestry, Louella Ballerino tied extra yarn into the warp loops. She tied the yarns in groups, regrouped them and tied again, and regrouped to the original position for a final tieing (Plate 122).

A weaver is bound to be on the lookout for odd objects to weight and enhance a tapestry. Junk shops, boat yards, hardware stores and old tool sheds yield unexpected treasures. Marian Sanders found just the right objects (none of us knows *what* they are) to finish off her brown and black and white, very textured hanging (Plates 123 and 124).

All but one of the weavings by our own group in this book have the warp running vertically, up and down. If the warp as it hangs seems too

116. Tree tapestry by Christine Cook is stretched to its full width on a concealed wood hanger.

117. Detail shows how to sew wood strip to back of tapestry and through warp loops, to hang it.

118. Wrapped warp extends the size of Jean Robinson's little tapestry, "Tide Pool". At top, it loops over driftwood hanger; at bottom, it drops to stoneware beads used as weights.

119. A twig, pushed through warp loops at top of Tess Goldsmith's "Jubilee", makes an appropriate hanger. The weights at the bottom are bleached, dyed turkey neck bones (see Color Plate 6). Collection of Mr. and Mrs. Stephen Nemetz.

120. Blue warp is threaded through blue beads in Helen Hennessey's "Off and Away" tapestry. Warp is wrapped below the beads with yellow-green thread, securing extra yarns for fringe.

121. Mahogany hanging bar at top of Helen Hennessey's tapestry is drilled with holes; a cord runs along the top threading through warp loops, pulling warp tight against bar.

122. Extra yarn is knotted into warp loops in Louella Ballerino's hanging and tied to make a patterned fringe.

thin, the weaver adds to it by tying in more yarn. The exception to vertical warping among our tapestries is the child's drawing of a horse by Celia Wagner (Plate 103). The weaving from Harrania by the Egyptian children (Plate 70) also has the warp running horizontally. This is true of many tapestries done in Europe and is probably why we seldom see fringe on the bottom of contemporary European tapestry.

Whether or not one wants fringe is a purely personal decision and each tapestry is a separate problem to solve.

124. *Unusual objects weight the ends of long wrapped warp in Marian Sanders' brown and black with white tapestry. Note the variety in textures of yarn and weaves.*

123. *Detail of found objects Marian Sanders discovered and used to finish her tapestry.*

89

125. *The banjo bag, designed by Lois Renwick, is woven in one piece. It uses a great variety of materials in the off-white-beige-brown range.*

11
Special Project:
Banjo Bag

Using eccentric warping, Lois Renwick designed and wove a banjo-shaped bag or tote which we think has all the ideal features. The handle won't pull out or twist out of place because it is woven in. The bag is roomy, the material durable. It's easy to weave and handsome.

Make the loom for this bag out of hardboard 40 inches long; the circular part is 13 inches in diameter. Reinforce the handle area with a strip of wood on the back (Plate 126). First warping runs the full length of the loom to make the handle. It is woven before the round areas are warped. The Egyptian knot makes a sturdy weave for the handle (Plate 127).

With the handle finished, begin the eccentric warping across the body of the purse at each end of the loom. Lois used a hard linen for the warp. As soon as she laid down one area of eccentric warping, she buttonholed it tightly in the center (Plate 128). She added another area of warping at right angles to the first and buttonholed it tightly. This buttonholing permits a view of the woven handle beneath, giving dimension to the work.

Next, Lois slipped a round ring under the buttonholed area and laid in additional warp from the edge of the purse around the ring and back to the edge. Using the ring lessens the amount of warp that would otherwise cross the center area (Plate 129).

Jute, cowhair, goathair, linen and rug yarn were woven into the warp, using both plain weave and Egyptian knot to give additional texture (Plate 130).

To complete the bag, Lois wove a boxing strip separately, sewing it between the two halves when the bag was removed from the loom. She used heavy canvas to line it. A zipper closing might be used—sew it into the lining along the straight top edge (Plate 125).

126. Masonite loom for banjo bag is 40"
long; handle area is reinforced with wood strip.

127. Handle area is warped first and
woven with Egyptian knot, for strength.

128. *Eccentric warp (about 14 strands) for body of bag is buttonholed in the center. A second warping will be done at right angles to the first.*

129. Round ring under
buttonholed area holds
remaining warp for the
bag and permits a view
of woven handle below.

130. Bag is woven around and around on circular loom, using a great
variety of materials. To complete bag, a separate boxing strip is
woven and sewed to circular shapes when they are removed from the loom.

12

Weaving a Jacket on a Foam Form

A block of plastic foam makes an excellent loom for woven projects that require a special shape—a jacket for instance. You can cut it any shape you want with a sharp knife or hot wire (heat a coat hanger on the range burner, handle with oven mitts). Don't worry if the cut edge is not perfectly smooth—a bit of irregularity does not matter.

Plastic foam has other advantages too. Pins you stick into it stay where they are placed. You can draw your design directly onto the block. It is easy to handle because it is so light in weight.

One disadvantage of plastic foam is that it will chip out if you put too much stress on the pins or nails stuck into it. Some weavers use masking tape along the pin lines to overcome this. Others cover the block with an old linen towel or muslin sheeting. In that case you draw your design on the fabric covering with a felt tip pen.

Frances Patten used a plastic foam loom for weaving her jacket in jewel-tone colors. She

tapered the sides gradually so that the form is slightly wider at the bottom than at the shoulders. The shoulders are cut on a slant to fit her body (Plates 131 and 132). Use your favorite dress or coat pattern to trace the slope that is best for you. In most patterns, this drop is about an inch from neck to armhole.

To warp the loop, stick card- or T-pins (Plate 133) on top of the shoulders about ¼ inch apart (Plate 134). Then stick a row of pins around the neckline about ¼ inch apart—both front and back. Wrap the warp over the shoulder first—around and around the block. When you get to the neck front, thread the warp around the pin, down around the bottom, up the back to a back-of-the-neck pin, then return again to the bottom and up the front (Plate 135).

To add extra warps under the arm (down the edge of the plastic foam) use a weft thread as a knot bearer and tie the new warps to it (Plate 136). You now can weave the jacket from center front right, around the back, then to center front left (or vice versa) with one continuous

131. To make a jacket loom, cut the form from a block of plastic foam at least 1" thick. Draw the weaving design directly onto foam.

132. Cut form longer than jacket so warp threads at bottom can be used for fringe.

133. T-pins used for spacing warp are available in stationery stores.

134. Stick the card- or T-pins along the shoulder ¼" apart and wrap warp around and around the block.

135. Pins around the neckline are ¼" apart and warped from front down to bottom, then up to back neck pin—back and forth.

136. Use a weft thread as a knot bearer for carrying underarm warps.

weft. When Fran completed the weaving, she cut the warps along the bottom of the jacket and knotted them into fringe (Plates 139 and 140).

I admired Fran's jacket so much that I decided to weave one for myself. A word of caution here: In making mine I discovered that it is disastrous to pull the warp too tight. If you do, the pins cut through the plastic foam and shift position —especially around the neckline. Most beginners warp everything too tightly, forgetting that warp tightens up with the weaving. It should not be so loose that it is baggy on the surface of the loom but neither should there be tension on the pins that hold the warp at the neckline. If you warp a slab of plastic foam and decide you need to loosen the tension, you can cut the warp at the bottom edge and tie in more warp. Or simply cut notches along the bottom that the warp can slide into, to ease the tension.

97

137. Pin front edges of jacket onto block as you weave to get design and color match on both sides and to keep edges from pulling in.

I also found that I needed to be careful to go over and under *each warp* at the neckline. If two warps are treated as one, the warp can slip down into the finished weaving when the pins are removed.

It helped to pin the front edges of the jacket to the plastic block as I finished an area. This kept the garment from pulling in (Plate 137).

In some parts of my jacket, I used heavy rug yarn. In other areas I used odds and ends of knitting worsted. I also used some fine silk with slubs of heavier twist. In order to adjust for these varied weights of yarn, I doubled the knitting yarn, using two threads as one, and tripled the silk, using three threads in the needle.

To finish my jacket, I tied the warp ends two by two and threaded them into a needle after I had tied them together with a square knot. I then worked the tied ends back into the weaving on the wrong side (Plate 138).

My jacket colors are reds, oranges, magentas, golds and purple. I lined it with a smooth silk-like fabric in bright orange. I wear it with a wine-colored dress.

138. To finish jacket without fringe, tie warp ends with square knots and weave ends back into the wrong side.

139. "Butterfly Jacket" was woven by
Frances Patten on a plastic foam form in
the orange-red-magenta color range.

140. This jacket incorporates all the characteristics
and processes that we consider essential to great
needleweaving. It has a limited number of colors
but many tones and textures of each. It makes use of
the tapestry slit, the locked join and the dovetailed
join. It uses both simple and triangular hatching
and makes good use of the meandering weft, in both the
plain areas and the butterfly design.

*141. "Winter Sun", 18x33", by Esther Dendel
is a tapestry woven on a canvas stretcher loom.
It combines the Swedish knot with plain
weaving—in black, white and natural
yarns accented with slubs of unspun fleece.*

13

Weaving on a Canvas Stretcher

You can make an "instant loom" for needle-weaving from canvas stretchers—the kind that artists use for oil painting. They are readily available from any store that sells art supplies. These stretchers slip together easily—no need for special tools. They come in a large range of sizes—in pairs so you can change the size of your loom by varying one set of dimensions. All ends are mitered and notched for a good fit at the corners (Plate 142).

Use the figure eight motion for warping stretcher bars. This keeps the warp threads in order. To begin, tie the end of a ball of warp thread around one end of the assembled stretcher bars. Carry the ball of warp to the opposite end of the stretcher. Go over the wood and to the back side, then forward to the front and across to a spot next to the first thread. You now have made a figure eight because the threads cross in the center area (Plate 143).

A good way to remember how to lead the thread is to watch whether the warp is coming from the bottom or top of the bars. If it comes from under the bar, bring it to the top of the opposite end; if it is on top, take it to the bot-

tom of the opposite end. If you think of this as you work, all the warp threads will be crossed in a figure eight.

Some weavers mark the bottom and top of the stretcher bars at $\frac{1}{4}$-inch intervals, but we find it sufficiently accurate to gauge the spacing of the warps by eye. Do not fill the rectangle completely with warp. Space the warp as you wish, say one thread about every $\frac{1}{4}$ inch, but shove the first thread in from the edge of the frame a couple of inches so the frame will not be a nuisance when you weave. Leave the same space at the opposite side also.

When the warp is in place and spaced evenly, it is sometimes helpful to run a piece of masking tape across the ends of the stretcher bars to keep the threads from sliding. If the warp is quite taut, this is not necessary. It is almost impossible to describe how tight the warp ought to be. Experience will teach this. As a clue, we can say that if the warp is being stretched, it is probably too tight. If there is a noticeable slack in it, it is too loose for efficient weaving. But if the warp is too loose, you can roll up a piece of cloth and insert the roll between the warp and the

142. Canvas stretchers, in sizes of your choice, slip together easily to make a frame loom.

143. Warp stretcher-frame so threads cross in center to form a figure 8; insert cardboard and push crossed warps to the top.

stretcher bar.

When the back set of threads is brought together in one place with the front set, some tightening of the warp will take place. The weaving process also tightens up the warp. If you are doubtful about the tension, wrap only a few times around the stretcher bars and try weaving the back and front threads together experimentally. It is better to use a few moments trying out the warp than to have the difficulty later of weaving on an overly taut or overly slack surface.

If you hold the stretcher bars so you can look in between the warp threads, you will see where the cross of the figure eight is located. I insert a stiff cardboard below this cross and push this cross to the top of the loom (Plates 143 and 144). You then can weave the warp above the cardboard into straps that will hold a strip of wood or dowel from which to hang the completed weaving (Plate 145).

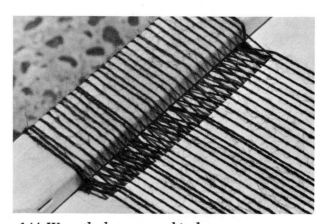

144. Warp the loom several inches away from both sides to give you working room.

145. Weave warp above the cardboard into straps, both front and back, before you start the body of the weaving.

102

146. *Finished tapestry (6x18″) is woven entirely with the Swedish knot; straps are done in plain weave. Colors are yellow-green, orange, red, magenta, deep purple.*

147. *To release the finished weaving, lift out a stretcher bar and the entire loom will come apart.*

148. *Use excess warp at bottom of hanging for fringe. Or use it to tie in extra yarn for a heavier effect.*

To make these straps, weave the warp on both the front and back sides of the stretcher bar. Weave the straps first, using the edge of the cardboard as a guide for how much weaving to do. Then remove the cardboard and bring all the warps below the straps together with a few rows of chaining or plain weaving. You are then ready to start the body of the weaving.

You will notice that if you have warped four threads to the inch, you have eight threads to the inch when the front and back warps are brought together. You may weave through all warps or you may want to use two warp threads as one, depending on the thickness of the weft. Usually, in parts of the weaving using fine thread or yarn, you will use every warp. In areas where you weave with heavier yarn, you may switch to using two warps together. You don't have to do it the same way throughout.

The unwoven warp at the bottom of the weaving is usually left for fringe. However it will appear meager unless additional yarns are tied into it (Plate 148). I like to add yarn to the fringe to repeat one or more of the colors in the weav-

103

149. Detail of Swedish knot moving from left to right.

150. Detail showing turn-around for Swedish knot and direction of weft from right to left.

ing. Cut each added yarn twice the length desired for the fringe. Thread one end through a needle and bring it through the weaving just above the last row that was woven. Pull the two ends even. Now use two warp threads (which usually are of a finer yarn) to wrap once again around the new yarn. Wrap the warp threads from opposite directions so they will be in position for pulling snug. Tie a square knot on the back side of the fringe, which is thus secured to the weaving. This method of finishing the weaving makes the fringe seem an integral part of weaving.

One of the advantages of using stretcher bars for a loom is that you can work from the back or wrong side if you wish and leave all the loose ends hanging. This is for weavings that will be seen only from the front.

Another reason why stretcher bars are excellent is that you can use the Swedish knot in the weaving. It is similar to the Egyptian knot, but it is worked from the wrong side of the weaving.

THE SWEDISH KNOT

The Swedish knot, worked from the back of the weaving, produces a rib on the right side. To make it, you work first from left to right by leading the weft over a warp thread and back under the same warp, pulling it snug. Now to the second warp thread, over it and back under.

If some weaving has been done before starting the Swedish knot, turn the frame so that when the Swedish knot is pulled tight, you are pulling the knot up to and down against what has been woven. Study Drawings 149 and 150 to see the difference in the slant of the thread going in each direction.

Working from right to left, the needle goes *up over* a warp (slant the needle in the direction of travel), then under the same warp (slant the needle back toward the area from which it came). One warp is now wrapped. Pull the weft down snugly against previous rows of weaving and move on to wrap the next warp.

The wrong side of the weaving (where you are working) will look like a knitted fabric (Plates 152 and 154). The right side will have ridges along the warp (Plates 151 and 153). On the right side, the weaving will appear almost exactly like the Egyptian knot which is done from the front of the loom.

I use the Egyptian knot when I am weaving on cardboard and the Swedish knot when I weave on stretcher bars.

Most right-handed persons find it easier to go from left to right than in the other direction. An

151. Swedish knot on right side of weaving forms ridges along warp, looks similar to Egyptian knot.

152. Swedish knot on back of weaving (the side you're working on) looks like knitting.

153. "Winter Sun" close-up shows textural variation you get by combining Swedish knot and plain weave, accented with the slubbiness of unspun wool.

154. Back view of "Winter Sun" shows knitted-like texture of the Swedish knot in contrast to areas of plain weave.

interesting texture is developed when you use one row of the Swedish knot from left to right and return the weft with a row of plain weaving. Then return with the Swedish knot from left to right, and back again with the plain weave.

If you experience some difficulty with the Swedish knot, the problem is usually the placement of the working weft in relation to the row of weaving. After each knot is completed, throw the thread that leads to the needle *above* the row of knots.

To summarize the Swedish knot: It produces a rib on the right side of the weaving and the rib runs in the direction of the warp. It completely wraps one warp thread (or two used as one). It is worked from the back of the weaving. It is worked above any existing weaving and each knot is cinched down against the previous row of weaving. If there is no existing weaving, the first row of Swedish knots may appear a little wobbly, but additional rows added above them will push them into shape. After each knot is cinched down, the working thread that leads to the needle or bodkin is thrown *above* the needle.

155. *"White Widow", 19x37", by Helen Hooper*
starts with bamboo scraps mounted on stretcher bars.
Web-like needleweaving fills the open areas.

14.

Weaving Your Loom into Your Work

Old barns, harness rooms and junk shops often provide treasures that have been overlooked by their owners. We tend to think of machine parts, harness gear and old boxes in terms of their former uses. But if we don't put this limitation on our imagination, these objects take on a beauty in their own right—the mellowness and character that comes with aging.

When these objects are used as a loom that becomes a permanent part of the needleweaving, we need to give thought to the kinds of materials that seem at home with old things. The spirit is one of earthiness rather than elegance. Shiny cords violate the essence of the old object to which we are trying to give a suitable new

setting. Jute, seine cord, horsehair, raffia, binder twine—these are the weaving materials that seem in character.

An old gate rescued from a chicken coop held nostalgic memories for Celia Wagner. The wood had aged to a silvery gray. The shape was pleasantly irregular. The design problem was what to do to the gate to enhance rather than detract from its charm. The solution was a design suggested by a torn fragment of a spider web, woven loosely in white crochet cotton (Plate 156).

To those who like their old wood highly polished, it may seem that hanging part of an old chicken coop door on the family room wall is either absurd or a "put-on". In this case it is neither. It is a sincere, imaginative act. It is a good example of the fact that an object does not need to be "pretty" to be beautiful. To members of the family and to some of the neighbors it speaks of old times remembered. To those coming upon it for the first time, it speaks of a way of life that is passing and of the beauty that sun and wind and time work into the fiber of old wood.

To make the spider web weaving, Celia drilled very small, inconspicuous holes in the door to anchor the main threads of the web. These warps are threaded and anchored on the back.

The spider was, after all, the original spinner and weaver. In the wild, a spider web seldom lasts more than a few days, so we feel justified in "capturing" some of these gossamer webs for study. To do this, we stand back about three feet

156. "Spider Web" of white crochet cotton enhances the weathered chicken coop door loom. Designed and woven by Celia Wagner.

157. Real spider webs can be captured for closer study—spray with white paint, lift onto black cardboard, affix with clear spray.

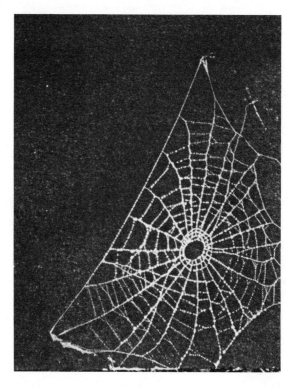

108

and spray the web with a fine mist of white paint from an aerosol can. This makes the pattern highly visible when we put a piece of black cardboard behind the web. Sometimes a few of the filaments that anchor the web to a bush have to be cut to release the entire web which then rests on the surface of the cardboard. To affix the web permanently we spray it with a clear acrylic (Plate 157).

The incredible beauty of the spacing, the surprise of sudden diagonals, the progression of sizes in rhythmic intervals lies before us ready for our response to the wonder of its craftsmanship.

Weavers do not act like Miss Muffet and scream when they see a spider. Instead they move closer to study the six spinnerets at the rear of the abdomen that control and shape the delicate silk filaments of the web.

The relationship of weavers with spiders goes back into the dim reaches of mythology. We recall the story of Arachne, the maiden skilled in weaving, who dared to challenge the goddess Minerva to a weaving contest and for her trouble was changed into a spider. Mythology condenses large truths into small stories.

But back to *our* weaving. The knots and loops that Celia Wagner used to weave and knot her spider web will be described in Chapter 15. We will look first at some other unique objects that make the loom a part of the weaving.

Joyce Barnes started with some pottery shards she found out on the desert. They were identified as belonging to an old Indian culture of our Southwest. So she needed something very special to combine with these ancient pieces of clay.

For a beginning, Joyce arranged five of the priceless shards in a vertical pendant with leather thongs (Plates 158 and 160). She felt this strand should hang in front of a somewhat sculptured background. For a hanging device, she found an old, rusted curved bit—the kind sometimes used for a horse with a sore mouth.

158. Antique pottery shards, held in place with leather thongs, are the center of interest in Joyce Barnes' weaving.

159. Detail of "one hand holds another" cording knot—Joyce Barnes combined it with weaving to add texture to shards hanging.

109

160. *Completed weaving of shards and an old curved bit loom is by Joyce Barnes.*

161. *Back view of "shards on a curved bit" exposes hawk and pheasant feathers incorporated into the weaving. Stoneware beads weight the fringe.*

162. Bent fragment of sea-washed copper mounted on driftwood is the loom Celia Wagner warped with green linen thread—and considered the composition complete.

Joyce repeated the curve of the bit with more strands of thong and tied coarse brown rug yarn on the thongs, both front and back.

She knotted and wove more rug yarn and coarse black horsehair in narrow strips, building around a flat piece of weaving in the center. For this, Joyce used the cording knot that we call "one hand holds the other" (Plate 159). You need two yarns to make this knot. Hold the left yarn in the left hand. With the right hand pick up the right yarn of the pair and make a buttonhole stitch (half hitch) with it. Now hold the right yarn taut and make a buttonhole loop

around it with the left yarn. Continue in this way. The purpose of the knot is to give added texture to yarns.

On the back side of the shard weaving, Joyce used feathers from a hawk and from a female pheasant. Some of the brown yarns hang free and are neither knotted nor woven. A few hand-formed stoneware beads weight the bottom of the hanging (Plate 161).

This hanging is a good example of a happy marriage between knotting and weaving, of a relationship established between things which (until they are assembled together) have noth-

111

164. *Disintegrating piece of driftwood is held together with warping and a small patch of weaving, by Beulah Rollyson.*

163. *Bristlecone pine loom gets a lichen-like patch of weaving from Bici Linklater.*

165. *Anne Chezar followed the pattern of the wood grain when she wove on her driftwood loom.*

ing in common except an earthiness of color and materials. The horse bit seems to belong with the other materials, not as contrived cleverness but as a natural holder for what is hung from it.

Sometimes when you use a piece of harness or driftwood from which to hang yarns, it is difficult to hand-hold the warps and weave into them. I cut slits in one end of a strip of cardboard and insert a warp in each slit. This weights the warp, keeps warp threads in order and spaces them evenly.

Another method of handling this problem is to tie the bottom ends of the warp to a dowel rod. The dowel may be left in or be removed when the weaving is finished. During the weaving it serves as a weight to keep the yarns taut. If it is not heavy enough in itself, tie small stones to it.

As an exercise in sensitivity training, our group focused on a summer project of needle-weaving-into-found-objects. The goal was to do *as little as possible* to display and quietly enhance the object. Sensitivity grew as we developed the feelings about when to stop. If any weaving we did detracted from the natural beauty of the object, we knew we had gone too far. In other words, if the weaving became more important than the natural "loom", what had been done was not the right thing to do.

Celia Wagner found a bent fragment of old green copper which had been cast up by the sea. She mounted it on driftwood only slightly larger than the metal. She used green linen thread to warp through holes that were already in the copper. When this was warped, it seemed that the warp threads were there to hold the copper in place and that no weft was needed. It is warped, but not woven and considered complete (Plate 162).

Bici Linklater brought a piece of bristle-cone pine that had branched, grown apart and merged again, separating finally into two rabbit-ear tips. We decided that the only weaving that could be done on this without overdoing it was a lichen-like patch in the center hole. The yarns are green-gold and gold-green and have a faint, lichen-like fuzz (Plate 163).

Beulah Rollyson brought some driftwood from a Minnesota trip. It had almost disintegrated from weathering so she notched it slightly on the ends to receive the warp. The warp actually holds the wood together. The weaving on it is minimal (Plate 164).

Anne Chezar followed the pattern of the grain already present in her piece of driftwood. After she had decided where she wanted the warps, she drilled tiny holes to receive them. The weaving is so natural looking that you have to look twice to be sure it did not grow there (Plate 165).

Sometimes when weaving on a punky piece of wood, you can insert pins directly into the soft wood to warp around. After the bit of weaving is finished, remove the pins and fasten the small weaving to the wood with fabric glue.

I never pass a piece of branched driftwood without wondering whether I would like to warp it and weave on it. The same is true of a pruned-off tree branch. Since a Christmas tree is usually chosen for its beauty of shape, a little judicious pruning after it has dried out turns it into a loom that challenges the weaver. Roméo Reyna did just that to produce the woven tree you see in Plates 167 and 168.

Old weathered boxes, or boards from them, make wonderful looms—especially if the ends are notched to fit into other notches at the corners of the box. Rosita Montgomery found a board from such a box and used the notches as spacers for her warp. The warp goes across the board, behind the first little extension of wood, out again on front of the board and across the loom. She started without any preconceived notion of what she would weave into the warp. She "felt out" the weaving pattern as she went along (Plate 166).

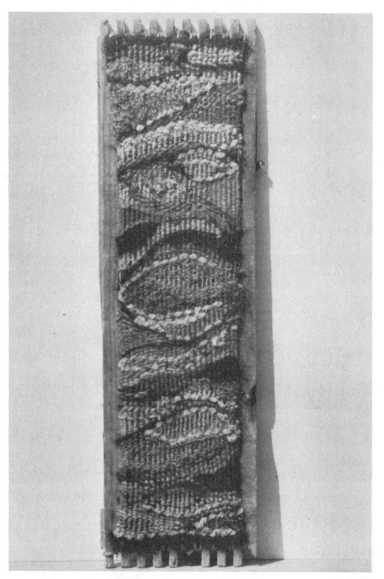

166. *Dovetail notching on an old weathered board is perfect for spacing the warp. Rosita Montgomery wove a free-flowing design on it.*

167. *"African Village" is the title for a tapestry Roméo Reyna wove on the bare branches of his Christmas tree loom. Hot sunny colors are dramatically emphasized when photographed against the cool background of the sea.*

168. *"African Village" detail shows close-up of weaving on bare branches of tree.*

169. Rusty tines of a pitchfork make a perfect loom for the cobweb-like weaving by Beth Brownlee.

A hame, one of the two curved wooden or metal pieces of harness which fit around the neck of a horse and to which the traces are attached, makes a graceful form from which to hang warp threads. A singletree, or whiffletree as it is sometimes called, is another attractive form. Many children growing up in cities or suburbs today never have seen a hame or singletree and have no idea of the harnesses that were used with draft horses. These items, like the chicken coop door, are manifestations of another time, though recently passed. It is good to preserve them in a beautiful and useful way.

The fork part of a pitchfork is in the same class and seems a natural loom for a weaving. Beth Brownlee started with rusty tines for her

*170. Two hoops soldered at right angles to one
another form a three-dimensional loom for
Celia Wagner's weaving. It casts an interesting
shadow pattern as it turns in the breeze.*

wall hanging (Plate 169).

Turning now from the old and the natural to looms that you make especially for needle-weaving, we will look at Celia Wagner's three-dimensional loom. It started with two metal hoops soldered together at right angles to each other. Then she wrapped the hoops with yarn (Plate 170). You can see weaving inside the hoops through the loosely spaced outside weaving as the mobile turns in the breeze.

By using round wire or brass stripping, all sorts of exciting forms may be soldered together to make the loom that will also frame or support the finished needleweaving.

Helen Hooper's "White Widow" began with a handful of bamboo strips from a factory that uses them to weave window blinds (Plate 171). Some of the bamboo is flat, some small and round like matchsticks. Helen began with these strips, arranging them this way and that.

She was not thinking of any definite design because she wanted the *material* to lead her toward a decision about what to do. When she had built some crisscross patterning, it seemed too heavy and dense, so she began to think about leaving open areas. When the proportion of open and solid seemed pleasing, she glued the pieces onto a rectangle of stretcher bars behind the bamboo and covered by it.

Helen drilled small holes in the bamboo so she could pull the warp across the open areas. The bamboo had been painted white before it came into Helen's possession. Since her home is adobe with natural-finish wood against which white is a handsome accent, she decided not to repaint the bamboo and to continue with white warp and white textured threads for the weft. The idea of weaving in a spider web-like pattern grew more or less accidentally from the way the warp crossed the open areas (Plate 172).

In deciding on a frame, it seemed important to emphasize the feeling of lightness. To enhance this she held the frame away from the edges with little posts made of dowels. The frame is made of four plain pieces of thin wood, mitered at the corners and painted white (Plate 155).

Perhaps the most natural of all objects on which to string warp and weave is another piece of fabric. (The possibilities of just this one type of weaving would fill another book.) The example we show is a hanging that combines needleweaving and embroidery on top of an upholstery fabric (Plates 173 and 174). The appeal of this hanging by Marian Sanders is in the variety of textures she achieved with white and nearly-white yarns on a light background. The finished hanging is mounted over plywood.

171. "White Widow" by Helen Hooper uses bamboo
scraps as foundation for the loom. These
pieces of both flat and matchstick bamboo are
glued to canvas stretchers in a lattice-like design.
Dowels separate frame from the composition—
this adds to the feeling of airiness.

172. "White Widow" detail of needleweaving that
fills the open spaces in the bamboo composition. Helen
threaded the warp through small holes drilled in
some of the bamboo pieces—and through openings in the
lattice design. The way the warp crisscrossed in
the open areas suggested the spider web-like weaving.

173. Fabric is the most natural of all objects on
which to string warp and weave. Marian Sanders
combines needleweaving and embroidery in her
wall hanging design on upholstery material.
It is mounted over plywood or hardboard.

174. Weaving-on-fabric detail shows the interesting texture and shadow pattern you get by using a variety of white and nearly-white yarns on an off-white background. The design uses plain weaving, wrapped warps, Roméo stitch, chaining and buttonholing.

*175. "Fish", 17x27", by Virginia Tiffany uses blue,
turquoise and green threads over a green fabric background
with a circle of gold foil crossed by orange threads.*

122

15

Locked Knot—the Roméo Stitch

The stitch that Celia Wagner used to secure the interstices of the spider web design on her chicken coop door is a useful but little-known way of locking threads precisely. It is used in parts of the world where needle lace is still being made. We found it in one of our stitchery books under the title of "Antwerp Stitch Edging". In our group we call it the "Roméo Stitch" because Roméo Reyna taught it to us and showed us how to use it in needlewoven tapestries.

Roméo tells us that he learned the stitch from Mexican field hands. He saw them play with string from potato sacks on rainy days when they could not get into the fields, and this stitch or knot was one of the things they made with the string—without needles, using only nimble fingers in a playful way.

The Roméo stitch is actually a knot worked into a buttonhole stitch. Any existing warp may be the foundation for this stitch. The needle passes behind the loop of the buttonhole stitch and over the working thread that leads to the eye of the needle. The needle must always point in the direction one is traveling with the work.

Work the second row of buttonhole knots halfway between each loop of the first row. While going back, the needle must point in the opposite direction because the work is traveling in the opposite direction (Drawing 177).

If the buttonhole stitch is made without knotting it, you have a knotless netting. Part of Celia Wagner's spider web was made by this method (Plate 176).

A variation of the Roméo stitch is to introduce the second row and each successive row *into the knot of the above row* instead of into the space between the knots. All sorts of variations in spacing the loops may be worked out for variety.

Sometimes the easiest way to use the locked knot or Roméo stitch is to draw the main lines of a design on cardboard and couch a yarn or thread along these design lines. The locked stitch is then worked within the areas outlined. A curved needle will get under the couched-

176. To duplicate Celia Wagner's spider web, you need to master the locked knot—which we call the Roméo stitch.

down threads easily. As each row of locked stitching approaches the couched outline it is knotted around the outlining thread. This keeps the whole thing together when it is removed from the cardboard. When the weaving is finished, snip the thread used for couching at the *back* of the cardboard. This releases the work on the front of the cardboard. The illustration we show is of a yoke in process designed by Jean Stange (Plates 178 and 179). When the

knotting is finished the yoke will be released from the cardboard and applied to a linen dress.

The couching is exactly like couching in embroidery except that the couching thread goes down holes in cardboard instead of going up and down in fabric. The thread that is being anchored lies flat on the cardboard and the couching thread goes over it before it returns to the back. If couching is new for you, look again at Plate 102.

177. Roméo stitch detail shows how to knot buttonhole stitch on existing warp (top); how to add second row between each loop of the first.

178. Yoke design by Jean Stange is traced on cardboard, then outlined with couching stitch and filled in with the locked stitch.

179. Yoke detail shows how locked stitches are knotted around the couched outlining. To release finished yoke, snip stitches on back of cardboard.

The Roméo stitch and knotless netting may also be used without cardboard or the couched-down thread, but it is a little more difficult to control without a rigid backing. The artist who made a contemporary technique of this is the Czech craftsman, Luba Krejci. (Her work is on exhibit in the textile department of the Art Institute of Chicago and in many other museums.) Luba Krejci's work is meant to be seen hanging away from the wall so that the shadows of the threads and the solid areas on the wall behind the work become part of the composition.

Judy Whelan used this technique in two of her screen panels (Plates 180 and 181).

Virginia Tiffany used a modified version of the uncouched and knotless netting in her "Fish" composition—in combination with couched and crisscross stitching on the background (Plates 182, 183 and 184).

180. A panel in Judy Whelan's screen uses a meandering locked stitch in one of the multi-colored mandalas (Color Plate 11).

181. Another panel in the mandala screen combines locked button-hole stitch with wrapped warp threads.

182. "Fish" panel by Virginia Tiffany shows use of locked knots and knotless netting combined with couching and crisscross stitching.

183. "Fish" detail—shadows cast by knotting become a part of the composition.

184. "Fish" detail shows circle of gold foil attached to background with orange crisscross stitches before knotting the fish design in greens and blues.

127

SOURCES OF SUPPLIES

There are so many yarn shops scattered over the United States that we cannot begin to list them all. What we have tried to do is list a supplier in each area of the country who will accept mail orders from individual customers.

Contessa Yarns
P.O. Box 37
Lebanon, Ct. 06249

Countryside Handweavers
P.O. Box 1743
Estes Park, Co. 80517

Craft Yarns of R. I., Inc.
603 Mineral Spring Ave.
Pawtucket, R.I. 02862

Denwar Craft Studios
236 E. 16th St.
Costa Mesa, Ca. 92627

Lily Mills
Shelby, N.C. 28150

Mexiskeins
Sharon Murfin
P.O. Box 1624
Missoula, Mt. 59801

The Yarn Depot
545 Sutter St.
San Francisco, Ca. 94102

185. Collar and cuffs by Helen Hennessey— woven in a neutral range from beige to brown, in spun and unspun yarns; appliquéd to linen dress. Detail shows wrapped warp.